THE FREE PRESS

New York   London   Toronto   Sydney   Singapore

The

PATRIOT

An Exhortation to Liberate
America from the Barbarians

GARY HART

THE FREE PRESS
A Division of Simon & Schuster Inc.
1230 Avenue of the Americas
New York, NY 10020

Manufactured in the United States of America

10 9 8 7 6 5 4 3 2 1

Designed by Carla Bolte

Library of Congress Cataloging-in-Publication Data

Hart, Gary
    The patriot : an exhortation to liberate America from the
barbarians / Gary Hart.
       p.   cm.
    ISBN 0-684-82751-4
    1. Political leadership.   2. Democracy.   3. United States—
Politics and government.   I. Title.
JC330.3.H37   1996
303.3'4'0973—dc20   96-10973
                                         CIP

Fortune has decided that I must speak about the state.
—*Niccolò Machiavelli, 1513*

Contents

CONTENTS

CONTENTS

The Patriot

A letter to the leader

*It is not possible for me to make a better gift than to offer
you the opportunity of understanding in the shortest time all
that I have learnt in so many years, and with so many
troubles and dangers*[1]

H AVING OBSERVED YOUR DRAMATIC RISE TO
national prominence and respected the
personal qualities which have produced it, I am honored
to accept your request to comment at some length on the
current political crisis of trust now shackling America,
on the qualities of character in a leader necessary to overcome it, on means of avoiding corruption by collapsing
political structures, and on measures necessary to create
a new sense of national interest, identity, and purpose.

   This task is made more urgent by the rapid decline of
confidence by the people in their leaders—caused prin-

cipally by the loss of confidence by the leaders in the people—and it is made more fortuitous by your emergence on the national scene as a new kind of leader not corrupted by current political cynicism, but one who is motivated solely by authentic patriotism and an idealistic commitment to national renewal.

It is as important as it is painful to acknowledge both the breadth of public despair over the sad state of governance in America and the depth of cynicism toward national leaders. The exigencies of the Cold War, especially in the form of the Vietnam conflict and its twin the Watergate scandal, produced a novel phenomenon: national leaders so distrusting of the people that they feared to tell them the truth. The mystical and sacred bond of trust, so central and indispensable to the proper functioning of a healthy republic, was breached. Predictably, the people responded with measurable increase of distrust in political leaders and the increasingly corrupt political system that produced them.

This is not a natural state for Americans. Always skeptical about politicians and their manipulations, we have seldom fallen prey to the distrust evidenced by older republics. But in my mature lifetime, all has changed. Political careerists mask the truth with simplistic slogans and glossy rhetoric; political consultants conceal their candidate's shortcomings behind vicious attacks on their opponents; officials prefer to communicate in the political polyglot of the paid lobbyist than in the direct language of ordinary citizens; and the political journalist, finding personal exposés more lucrative than issues of public governance, participates in this elaborate dance of distrust.

The fortunes of particular politicians are inconsequential. At risk is the survival of our national identity, the integrity of our communities, and the preservation of worthy cultural values—in short, the survival of authentic patriotism. The citizen's natural instinct of dedication to the national good is devalued by careerist politicians, money-changers in the temples of government, radical ideologues and twisted survivalists. Young Americans demonstrate justified suspicion of those false patriots today who preach love of country most loudly.

You have proved different. As a scholar, you have demonstrated an appreciation for the lessons of history. As a concerned citizen, you have led efforts to reform your political party and force it to abandon old arrangements favoring special constituencies. You have sought to create new institutions to address the needs of those without means and to educate children. And you have undertaken bold measures to restore the proper balance between humanity and our natural habitat. All are praiseworthy in a new leader and, together with your dedication to break money's stranglehold on governance, set you apart from the rank and file of ordinary, traditional politicians. These qualities must always be nurtured, but in ways that do not isolate you from peers and public.

Your greatest personal challenge is therefore to use your talents to master a system whose current characteristics you do not share.

The fundamental question you have raised with me—whether these characteristics qualify you for a dramatically different kind of national leadership—is the central question addressed in this brief work. It is a question less about you and more about our nation. Have we become too cynical for leadership guided by moral authority and idealism? Do we have, or should we have, a distinctive national purpose? If so, what sets us apart from other nations? Can we recapture our sense of patriotism or national idealism? If so, toward what cause? Do we grasp the historical hinge on which our times now swing at the end of the Cold War and at the dawn of a new millennium? And do we fully understand the unique, historic opportunities and dangers represented by the disintegration of old social forms and political structures around the world under the pressures of economic internationalism and expanding technology?

The answer to these and other monumental questions is, not fully enough. Thus, your great importance to our nation. And if not you, then someone like you who will break out of the old shopworn political systems and challenge the dormant sense of national greatness. Most Americans still feel that we should have a greater purpose, a mission of moral and historical consequence, an as yet unrealized national destiny. And they know it has to do with offering a hand of democratic friendship to peoples just shedding the oppressive totalitarian cloak and by demonstrating, by example more than sermon, the benefits of freedom and democracy. This places a greater obligation than ever before to practice democracy's highest ideals here at home, even greater than at the height of the Cold War. Creating a more perfect union—the premise of our Constitution—offers the greatest challenge and opportunity for a national leader in the emerging century.

These meditations are simply one American's ideas on how we may restore our national character through a renewed sense of national purpose. Take them for what they are worth. Throughout I have had recourse to certain recurring and unifying themes: the contrast between ancient and modern republics; the peculiar twentieth-century oscillations between left and right, especially concerning the creation and distribution of wealth; the related struggle between centralization and devolution of governmental powers; the vital distinction between benign and virulent nationalism; and the necessary tensions between social stability and political reform on the one hand and social reform and political stability on the other.

These meditations range widely because your challenge to me prompts them to and because they are pieces of an incomplete mosaic of the future of America. They begin with the framework of our government as a reminder of how our systems were shaped and how we became who we are. They continue by fixing the principles that should guide America's role as the principal power in a kaleidoscopic new world. They then come to focus on how we may create a new liberal nationalism, synthesizing the best principles of left and right, as a means of perfecting our own Constitutional promise of national unity. Finally, I have considered the attributes and qualities necessary to equip you for a unique kind of leadership that liberates the natural but dormant energies of civic virtue in the people. The aim of these essays and your leadership must be to create a *restoration* of cultural values, a *reformation* of political and social institutions, and a *renaissance* of national unity.

I have set the national interest above all considerations of partisanship, career or parochial concern. Rather than being an abstraction or a dangerous illusion, the national interest is both identifiable and transcendent. It is all that contributes to a secure, prosperous and civil society for the greatest number of citizens. It includes secure borders, a well-educated, healthy and productive citizenry, a robust and vigorous environment, streets and neighborhoods safe from violence, the security of the elderly, prudent public investment in the common good, a sound economy offering opportunities for workers and young people, care for the poor and needy, ethnic and racial tranquillity, and a wise and just government. That which contributes to these goals contributes to the national interest.

This work would represent the ultimate in arrogance and futility were it not for both your graciousness in inviting these disparate thoughts and your recognition of the unique experiences that may qualify me to offer them. You know my story. Like you, I was a citizen politician who came by force of circumstance, more than lifelong ambition, to seek national leadership. Like you, I stood outside and apart from those elements of my own party and the political system that, fearing the loss of their authority and power, resisted change and repressed reform. Like you, I believed there was a tangible, palpable beacon called the national interest that should be the sole guide for national policy. Like you, I believed that the founders of the American republic established a practical system of self-governance as a unique ideal that could only be tarnished by the practice of a more cynical *realpolitik* known to older states. In this principally I differ from my mentor Niccolò Machiavelli. For him, cunning, deviousness and trickery were among the tools necessary for the prince to achieve his purpose of creating a nation-state under secular authority and civil republican government.[2] That was then; this is now. The democratic leader, unlike the autocratic prince, is not separated from the people by class and position. His actions must reflect his purpose. He must not let a gap appear between his words and his deeds. He will not be perfect, for imperfection is the human condition. But he must be straightforward and candid, forceful and undeterred. Trickery may be used against a foreign enemy in the nation's interest, but it is never justified against the people in the leader's interest. In all these things and more, we think alike.

Some will be tempted to dismiss these reflections, on the ground that their author has been discredited, that having failed in my own leadership quest I am disqualified from advising others. Our society's blind worship of success assumes that only those who pass that ultimate test are worthy of attention and respect. In the eyes of many I did fail, through my own faults and errors, and am therefore disqualified from sharing in my nation's life and debate.

If so, it is a harsh penalty. For, in my own eyes, I *chose,* under intolerable conditions, not to be reduced from the status of a candidate to that of a media celebrity. I refused to participate in a culture which destroys leadership and demeans debate. The invasive and belittling scrutiny of political leaders, placing all their faults and failures on public display, is justified by the media as fulfilling their responsibility to protect the country from inferior leaders. Does anyone believe, since the media assumed this authority, that the caliber and quality of leadership has risen, that we have wiser, stronger, or more visionary leaders?

No. Rather, the media is waging a war, perhaps unconsciously, on political leadership and on that dignity that is essential to leadership. Their motives for this are complex and unclear, even to themselves. Some dislike the inequalities inherent in republican government. Some are driven purely by competitive commercial pressures. Some feel superior to the subjects they cover. Some resent authority. Some seek acclaim and professional reward. Few know their motives, but all should care, because our nation is at stake.

I refused to submit to a media inquisition that destroys leadership and to a celebrity culture that prefers sensational exposé to serious political discourse. It is a simple fact that we will have no great leaders while this irrational war continues.

My own efforts at reform have failed, and I may have abandoned hope of national leadership, but I have not abandoned hope that another might forge anew the bond of trust between citizens and leader by showing his confidence in the people, setting the country on a new course toward a new national purpose in which all can share. When learned from, failure can be a powerful teacher. For my exile, I am wiser; for my pain, I see more clearly; for my battles with the media inquisition and its twin the celebrity culture, I am stronger. There is one proof—these thoughts themselves. Careers can be crushed, but ideas endure. The ideas in this book are derived from a lifetime of learning.

Such I have tried to do in this work. I pray it may be of some use. By first reviewing a basic understanding of our novel experiment in government, we may apply our two-century-old experience to the chaotic world waiting on our doorstep and then return home to a house in need of serious restoration.

You have bestowed a great honor in asking me to conduct this idiosyncratic excursion into the American prospect. Take what may best serve you, and godspeed.

Notes

1. All epigrams at chapter headings are from *The Prince,* Niccolò Machiavelli.

2. ". . . it is necessary for a prince wishing to hold his own to know how to do wrong, and to make use of it or not according to necessity." *The Prince,* Niccolò Machiavelli. This "argument from necessity," so central to Machiavelli's amoral realism, has come to define Machiavellian in the popular mind and sadly has obscured his patriotic nationalism, a far greater contribution to Western political thought. Lost amidst the moralistic and often hypocritical condemnation of his methods is the sight of his loftier goals: the creation of an Italian nation-state, the recovery of the classic republican ideal, and the establishment of a benign secular, civil government under an ideal prince—a government above the corrupt alliances between monarchy and church which had dominated Europe for centuries. Indeed, for Machiavelli, the prince had great behavioral latitude before even beginning to approximate the greed, selfishness, and corruption of the pope and monarch. If our friend Nicco is cynical, he has good cause.

One marvels not at the cynicism he absorbed in his earlier diplomatic perambulations through the courts of warring city states, but rather at a higher idealism that survived—his belief in a greater possibility for Italy, a nobler kind of politics. I argue that, through the advances of enlightened Jeffersonian democracy, Machiavelli's *methods* are today both immoral and counterproductive to the highest end, a nation in which its own citizens have trust. Nixonian–Kissingerian recourse to these methods was hugely destructive of that trust which is democracy's natural cement. This work seeks to identify new methods to achieve Machiavelli's ultimate goals, idealistic patriotism and liberal nationalism.

Nº· I

Modern democracy and restoration of first principles

All states, all powers, that have held and hold rule over men have been and are either republics or principalities

THE TESTS OF DEMOCRACY IN THE TWENTY-first century will be whether it is able to unify its citizens absent a major threat; whether it can survive disintegrative economic, cultural, and political forces; and how it will generate new opportunities for its workers and young people. None of these objectives can be achieved by reliance on the antiquated policies employed during the Cold War or by resort to the tedious theology of current partisan quarrels. The great challenge of your generation is to make the abstract eighteenth-century notion of republican democracy vital to the diffuse, unfocused century just ahead. Therefore it is instructive to examine first principles to determine whether and how the original democratic ideal may be applied to the conditions of today, or whether a radical revision of our constitutional process and complex distribution of power (imposing greater authority—and therefore responsibility—in the executive, imposing legislative term limits, and so forth) is required.

As in earlier times, the world is divided between a variety of forms of democracies and a variety of forms of dictatorship. Concern is not given here to any detailed consideration of the various forms of dictatorship, whether authoritarian or totalitarian. It is important only for the new leader to have a thorough knowledge of the nature of dictatorship and the style of the dictator so that he will not be taken unawares in affairs of state.[1] In this century we have faced Hitler, Stalin, Kim Il Sung, Pol Pot, and Saddam Hussein, to name only a few of the despots who operated either in their own names or through the conglomerate tyranny of a party.

It is also appropriate to inquire whether it is ever justified for a democratic leader to use the tyrant's or dictator's methods against him. I suggest that if his opponent is converted to tyranny, a tyrant succeeds. Rather, isolation, through refusal of diplomatic recognition, embargo, and commercial barriers, suffices for those whose brutality remains within their own borders.

Collective international military action, as in the 1991 Persian Gulf war, is sometimes required against those who invade their neighbor's territory. And unilateral military action is called for against those who threaten the legitimate interests or attack the citizens or property of the United States.

Principally, however, here we are concerned with leadership in political systems dependent on the public franchise and the nature of leadership required to govern in systems that incorporate the ancient traditions, ideas and practices of the republic with the egalitarian principles manifested so forcefully in the revolutionary movements of the late eighteenth century.

The United States is the oldest and most visible constitutional democracy, and the United Kingdom is the oldest and most imitated of the parliamentary democracies. Both types of democracy rely on an independent judicial branch to interpret and enforce its laws. Modern democracies of both types are republican; that is, they rely upon open and free elections and require the periodic selection of representatives to enact such laws as the people at large may desire. Neither democratic system, though, provides complete citizen satisfaction. Many in parliamentary democracies argue for constitutions and separation of executive and legislative powers. Some in constitutional systems such as ours argue for parliamentary democracy, making legislative majorities more responsible for administration of government.

Much of this disquiet is attributable to inefficiencies inherent in democratic government. Eighteenth-century philosophers of democratic theory, concerned with concentrated autocratic power, set out to disperse it and by so doing guaranteed inefficiency.[2] Moreover, consensus does not flourish where dissent is exalted.

The United States, the oldest and most stable of two-party democracies, faces either emergence of new parties or realignment of old ones at the close of the twentieth century. Multiple-party systems normally require a postelection consensus on major issues and negotiation of power sharing before a government is formed, thus establishing a stable basis of governance subject to disruption only by the emergence of new crises. Our current two-party system—featuring increasing factionalism within both parties—when combined with separation of powers between executive and legislative and the potential for different parties occupying each branch, can only become more complex if additional parties emerge. It is much more likely that current party factions will realign themselves into two fundamentally different parties, as occurred at the beginning of both the nineteenth and twentieth centuries.

But regardless of party structure, the secret of wise government in the twenty-first century will be the design of new definitions for new national challenges— thereby confounding all those who have defined themselves by the stakes they have invested in old debates—and in forming new bases for consensus absent stale ideological quarrels.[3] The ills of modern American democracy do not reside in its constitutional structures and institutional framework. Rather they can be found in the political parties, their ideologies and candidates, and the network of interests that seek always to influence their behavior. All are too selfish, too narrowly focused, too orthodox and rigid, too partisan and empty of ideas. The people seek unity of action and purpose, and all about them is division and partisanship. Such flaws as exist in today's American politics—and they are consequential—find no roots in the doctrine of separation of powers, the federal system, the Bill of Rights, or other constitutional bedrock. It is in the nature of inadequate political leaders to seek systemic causes for their own personal shortcomings. The fault is not in our Constitution, but in ourselves.

American democracy will be made to work effectively in the twenty-first century if you are able to replace today's narrow interests with the unifying cause of leaving to our children a better nation than we found: in short, one characterized by the national interest as defined at the outset of this work.

Notes

1. The most obvious examples of dictatorship in modern memory include Joseph Stalin—with whom Western leaders, including American presidents, had to deal as an ally during World War II—and his successors—with whom subsequent Western leaders had to deal as adversaries thereafter. Those most successful in this enterprise were those who comprehended the totalitarian mentality most clearly (see Number Four). But today, of the two dozen conflicts in the world, no more than one or two involve a state, whether tyrannical or not. Most conflicts are between or among tribes, religious clans, or gangs. In these, as we should have learned in Somalia, we can have little unilateral effect.

2. Most notable of these was James Madison, whose theories of competing—and therefore balancing—interests played such a powerful role in structuring the United States Constitution.

3. An important instance of this is redefinition of the meaning of national security in the aftermath of the Cold War (see Number Eleven).

Concerning democratic republics and national renewal

He who would keep a city accustomed to freedom will hold it more easily by the means of its own citizens than in any other way

T HE NEXT GREAT NATIONAL LEADER WILL BE one who successfully exhorts elites, narrow interests, and old power structures to adopt an agenda for national renewal as their policy and the nation's interest as their standard. The democratic ideal will be reawakened by this new leader, who inspires all citizens to participate in the governance of their community and national lives. Not to have taken part in the affairs affecting one's nation is to risk not having fully lived.

From the time of Machiavelli through the democratic revolutions of the late eighteenth and early nineteenth centuries, and onward until the end of the colonial period of the mid-twentieth century, it was generally assumed that people in bondage to corrupt oligarchies or remote monarchies had to throw off their chains by force. Even as enlightened a spirit as Jefferson could famously declare: "I hold it that a little rebellion now and then is a good thing" and "The tree of liberty must be refreshed from time to time with the blood of patriots and tyrants."

But American renewal requires no such physical rebellion or bloodshed, for our present chains are forged only by ourselves. Our "mind-forged manacles" preventing renewal are factionalism, prejudice, materialism, and preoccupation with amusement. Under a new leader, we will peacefully substitute for these manacles values of community, tolerance, deferred gratification, and authentic love of country.

An agenda for national renewal will include reform and renewal of the nation's core public structures, including foremost the public education system but also health, employment training, and public assistance programs. Social equity requires that each of these systems be made as inclusive as possible while focusing their resources on those most in need. Fiscal responsibility, which is vital to a sound economy, can only be assured by directing expenditures to those projects that strengthen and benefit the nation at large, not narrow or special interests, and by raising sufficient revenues, through simple and equitable taxes on consumption, to meet current expenditures. To assure accurate accounting, public budgets must distinguish between current expenditures and long-term capital investments required to maintain public infrastructures.[1]

The key to the future success of the American republic is renewed civic spirit and citizen participation. The American model for the responsible citizen—the Jeffersonian yeoman—assumes responsibility not only for his or her own family but also for the community and national commonwealth.

Whereas it is possible to have a republic that does not incorporate all the ideals of the democratic society, it is difficult to imagine a democracy that is not rooted in the classic republic. In general, citizens of republics have been inclined to delegate great expanses of power to representatives of propertied groups whether or not those groups actually represented the day-to-day concerns of the individual citizen. In many republics these powerful interests and their representatives came to constitute ruling elites and de facto oligarchies. There was an unspoken assumption that the good of the cultural and economic elites—such as the banking barons and industrial tycoons (the Morgans, Vanderbilts, Rockefellers, and so forth) of early twentieth-century America—represented the good of the republic. In contrast, the radical democratic ideals of the past two centuries have come to insist upon equal participation by all and equal representation of all, regardless of class, race, gender, or heritage.

Thus, in modern democratic republics, the egalitarian ideal is grafted onto the classic ideal of interest-group representation reflected in the republic. The leader in a democratic republic is therefore obliged to respond both to elites, representing concentrated power and wealth, and to the masses of enfranchised citizens, who do not see themselves as represented by elite power structures. As a new leader, you must take careful note that much of current-day popular discontent emanates from the people's sense that elite power structures are concerned with their own selfish interests more than the common good. Indeed, these so-called "special interests" are being served by government more than it serves the national interest.[2]

National renewal must be defined by those public policies that increase the talent, health, and well-being of the people at large, by investments that improve the public assets and infrastructure of the nation, by expenditures that achieve a legitimate level of national security, and by activities that liberate creative energies and enhance cultural achievement for the greatest number. This agenda is greater than the sum of the desires of all America's interest groups.

This agenda, though, requires citizen participation if a

transcendent interest of national renewal rises above the collection of narrow interests. We have lately become a nation motivated more by the pursuit of private interest in the short term than by the exercise of civic virtue in the interest of posterity. The surest way to assure a brighter future for our progeny is through collective as well as individual action and through public as well as private legacies. Citizen commitment to invest time and energy in pursuit of the public good is also the surest guarantee that government by special interest will give way to government in the national interest.

Notes

1. The concept of a capital budget to reflect accurately long-term public investment, as distinct from annualized expenditures, is one that I and others have long advocated. If the federal government were to adopt the sound principle of capital budgeting, as almost all businesses do, our national deficits would look much more reasonable.

2. This issue played a central role in my own campaign for national leadership in 1984 and has been a strong motivating force throughout my public life. It has been an article of faith, with considerable justification, that the Republican party would continue to represent powerful financial and industrial interests as in the past. But by the last quarter of the twentieth century, a multitude of constituencies that found a political home and voice in the Democratic party had *become* the party.

It was but a platform for a virtual cacophony of special-interest voices primarily seeking achievement of their own agendas, with the party having neither a unifying voice nor a greater national agenda of its own. I was convinced then, and remain so today, that the Democratic party will become a permanent minority party or give way to a new party unless it rediscovers its progressive-reform mantle in the interest of national renewal and thus become something greater than a collection of its constituent parts.

Nº. 3

Concerning cultivation of new democracies and achievement of the common good

Nothing makes a prince so much esteemed as great enterprises and setting a fine example

T HE MODERN DEMOCRATIC LEADER HAS proved more proficient at unifying his fellow citizens against a common enemy, whether at home or abroad, than toward a common good.[1] Now, there being no single, unifying common enemy, you have for your greatest task the generation of national unity absent an external demon. Indeed, you must carefully and patiently cultivate new democracies in the turbulent world of radical fundamentalism, competing trade blocs, and disintegrating belief systems in order to guarantee a world stable enough to permit a new era of national renewal at home.

None of these democratic experiments is more important to America and the world than the one under way in present-day Russia. Upon its success may hinge the stability of Western alliances and structures, as well as your ability to focus on the vital task of reforming democratic institutions in America in the twenty-first century. Russia's first elected leader since the brief Kerensky government, Boris Yeltsin, has the legitimacy and authority granted by a popular mandate. But that mandate was originally granted just after the disintegration of the Soviet empire and just before the collapse of a much more ancient Russian empire. He governs now as much by force of personality and will as by regularly ordered public enfranchisement.[2]

Yeltsin governs what is nominally a parliamentary democracy, but it is so in name only. The Russian parliament, a product of the *ancien régime,* is more representative of industrial interests and nationalistic groups than of the citizens at large. In the broadest terms, it is more republican than democratic. The institutions of modern democracy—broadly-based political parties, an independent judiciary, regular elections, public referenda, an autonomous legislature, a free and responsible press, public access to elected officials and the decision-making process—have yet to take root in Russia, though uneven progress is being made. The world's leading democracies have assisted only fitfully in the Russian democratic revolution. Regrettably, they have proved more successful at organizing to combat communist authoritarianism than at organizing to establish and strengthen democratic republicanism.

In considerable part these meditations explore why this is so and what can be done to rectify this shortcoming. They are written for you, the hope of a new generation, to reflect on the nature of leadership in an age that consumes leaders (and everything else) rapidly, and on the nature of governance at a time when great unifying enemies are as rare as great unifying leaders.[3]

If a leader is to be judged by the enemies he makes, a new leader may have before him the task of identifying worthy enemies. Compared to the certainty of the cold war, with its simplified, objectified adversary, the enemies of twenty-first century democracy will be more abstract and thus less subject to demonization.[4] You will face nuclear terrorists, renegade tribal leaders, local warlords, and fundamentalist fanatics. But the new threats— mass migration, ethnic grievance, trade wars, exploding populations, massive pollution—are less personalized and less subject to military resolution.

Democracy-building in Russia and other countries emerging from dictatorship can be a cause that allows you not only to unify the nation behind a common good but to substitute principle for interest in American foreign policy. This is not to suggest a necessary separation between principle and interest, but rather that democracy-building, in Russia and elsewhere, is the right thing to do and in the national interest. Following a century with two world wars, extended conflicts in Korea and Vietnam, and a far-flung U.S. military presence throughout Europe and Asia, your message that stable political and economic structures in emerging democracies are vital to national rebuilding in America will find resonance and widespread support.

Notes

1. History will reflect with considerable interest, and possible puzzlement, on the powerful role the "communist threat" played as a theme for national unity and sacrifice in the America of the 1940s to the 1990s.

2. But Yeltsin and/or other candidates for national leadership must face a genuine, though probably dispirited, public referendum on national leadership in the spring of 1996.

3. It was inevitable, now looking back, that processes of reduction, leveling, exposé, and journalistic commercialism would eventually consume leaders along with all else. An age of consumption devalues the products consumed, in this case leadership, and always looks for new products (or leaders) to replace them (see Number Twenty-Three).

4. Iraq's Saddam Hussein being a modest exception, most current threats to democratic stability are local and small-bore.

5. This is not to suggest a necessary separation between principle and interest, but rather that democracy-building, in Russia and elsewhere, combines what is right with what is expedient.

No. 4

*What lessons may be learned from the
past ideological century concerning
centralized political systems*

> *It cannot be called talent to slay fellow citizens, to deceive
> friends, to be without faith, without mercy, without religion;
> such methods may gain empire, but not glory*

BOTH TOO MUCH AND TOO LITTLE CAN BE
made of the successful but wrenching
struggle by Western democracies against communism.
Too little will be made if new leaders—your generation—readily forget the banal destructiveness of totalitarianism. Too much will be made if those who came to
love the struggle miss its clarity and therefore seek to
breath new life into this dead demon.

29

Communist ideology, and the age of political ideology in general, cannot be understood outside the context of twentieth-century political history. One must review this history to appreciate fully the continuing struggle between left and right and the parallel struggle between centralization and devolution of government power.

The decline of monarchical empires in the nineteenth century, especially the Austro-Hungarian empire, left a vacuum of belief in the Western world. Since benign nationalistic impulses were not yet strong enough to fill this vacuum, it was left to ideology to stir men's minds.

Socialism gave purpose and direction to working classes urbanized and organized during the early industrial age. Marx produced the theoretical framework for communism, socialism's more vivid extreme. Defeat in World War I left Germany vulnerable to communist influence; virulent nationalism assumed the face of fascism to counter this threat. The defeat of White Russian forces during the Russian civil war and the rise of Stalin thereafter threatened an expansion of the Bolshevik revolution into western Europe and greatly strengthened the hand of ultranationalists like Hitler. Thus the first of the great ideological struggles of the twentieth century began.

It would take a second great international war to bring the forces of democracy into this ideological struggle. In the meantime, Stalin brutally organized Russia and its historic empire into a state eternally on guard against counterrevolution and foreign influence. National security forces were used to suppress millions of Russians and minority ethnic groups. Autonomous peasant farms were eradicated. A closely inbred *nomenklatura* administered centralized authority: despite pro forma "elections" the Communist party held all power, and the people (in whose name the totalitarian revolution continued to be carried out) were denied any voice in their own affairs.

As midcentury approached, western Europe found itself menaced more by Hitler's Third Reich than by Stalin's communist revolution. For a brief, bloody moment the forces of democracy found it imperative to make common cause with Soviet communism to crush the fascist threat to both. Following Hitler's demise, though, the inevitable struggle between communist expansionism and Western democracy was quickly engaged. The invention of thermonuclear weapons, and the catastrophic consequences of their possible use, forced this struggle to be waged largely in the back alleys of former colonial capitals throughout Africa, Latin America, and Southeast Asia.

Stalin used the existence of Western military organizations (as Lenin had done following Western military intervention in the Russian civil war) to legitimize centralization of power in the Communist party and himself as its leader. The weapons Stalin used—brutality, fear, repression, and eradication, all prevalent in the totalitarian experience—are neither available nor desirable to the democratic leader. But they may be recalled during times of confrontation between forces of democracy and dictatorship to illustrate the seriousness of the threat to democratic systems posed by undemocratic opponents.

There are lessons for a new leader in the twentieth century's confused and turbulent ideological history and from the exercise of state power in pursuit of ideology. Both Hitler and Stalin concentrated power first in the state, then in themselves in the interest of totalitarianism. Both arguably did so to prevent national collapse. Franklin Roosevelt also greatly centralized state power: first to overcome economic depression, and then (along with other Western leaders) to combat the threat of fascism. The democratic nations combined their military power—also a function of strong centralized government—to contain and defeat communism.

Now all is changed. The communist threat having disappeared and the Western left having collapsed, forces of the right are resurgent in their demand for devolution of power—the dismantling of centralized government—except for the military. These forces range from the benign, those opposed to income redistribution and government regulation, to the virulent, militias, faintly reminiscent of early fascism, violently convinced that mysterious, undefined international interests have taken over the American government; in between are anti-immigrant, ethnically pure, rigidly nationalistic interests.[1] Americans, accustomed to two centuries of isolation from ideological tides, now find themselves swept up in the West's rightward shift.

Realization of national renewal is critically linked to an accurate interpretation of the national character— whether we are a mere collection of self-interested individuals (or, at best, tribes) or a true nation, a community with collective interests in prosperity, security, and the quality of our lives. This in turn requires an appreciation for the dilemma created by power and government in American history. In ancient republics power was dispersed among the many, the few, and the one (the people, the nobility, and the monarchy, respectively) to ensure political stability and to prevent constant flux caused by popular ("mob") rule. Jeffersonian democracy disperses power differently: the "ward" or grass-roots community was to be the locus of as much authority as possible. This was Jefferson's way of avoiding concentrated power and guaranteeing "revolution" or reform in every generation.[2]

The American right has now placed a starvation siege around governmental concerns with racial and gender equality, securities, environmental and workplace regulation, and social and community welfare, as well as other legacies of the Great Society of the 1960s and

GARY HART

New Deal of the 1930s. This cyclical counterreformation reveals much concerning the endless complexity of American political belief. Alexander Hamilton believed a strong central government necessary to protect and promote American commercial interests. Thomas Jefferson, though, feared the oppressive combined burden of central government power and concentrated wealth on the ordinary taxpaying citizen. It took a legatee of Jefferson, Franklin Roosevelt, to summon government power on behalf of the ordinary citizen. Now the heirs of Hamilton wish to restore the *status quo ante,* devolving authority over social policies as they wish to local and state governments and dismantling uniform national standards, but retaining the powers of the central government in the service of economic elites and powerful corporate interests.

This neo-Hamiltonian experiment will succeed until the next economic crisis summons a Rooseveltian government on behalf of the Jeffersonian common man and woman. The question you must ask the American people is how often this oscillation between social reform and counterreform must occur before we settle finally on one of three stable systems: a pure Jeffersonian vision of decentralized government and empowered citizens, the neo-Hamiltonian vision of a strong central government for the powerful few, or a Rooseveltian vision of a strong national government supporting our economic and security interests internationally and providing limited economic and social security domestically. If the fondest dreams of the current counter-reformers are realized, you must expect to face increased economic division, regional economic imbalances, restoration of corporate buccaneering, mounting environmental hazards, return of grandparents to the nuclear family, expansion of "gated-community" America, and institutionalization of private security forces. The return of these species from the ancient social forest will greatly complicate your task of national renewal.

Our nation is politically conservative, its policies—especially orthodox monetary doctrines—dominated by economic elites, and its people far from inclined to change for its own sake. Absent a depression or severe recession, the possibility of radical upheaval, mob rule, or mass action is remote. Excesses of democracy have rarely visited America. Institutional reform, in the absence of serious economic downturn, is unlikely. Thus any project of national renewal introducing new ideas and institutional reforms faces a deadly enemy in the status quo. Mutual distrust between leaders and people simply compounds this problem.

Conservative elites and a cautious public may prefer the *status quo,* but the world changes nonetheless. And the world is changing rapidly now, especially under the impact of information technology and global markets. Therefore you can harness the energies of the new information age and long-delayed generational reform,

even in this age of social regression, to create a new basis
for national renewal. Democracy cannot stand still; it is a
dynamo. Efforts to preserve it like a rare insect in amber
are doomed from the outset. Democracy is adaptive and
requires adaptation. At its best, democracy's peculiar genius is its constant harmonization of public action with
the realities of each new age. This adaptability accounts
for democracy's survival as the world's most durable
political ideology and America's survival as the world's
oldest democracy. The greatest apostle of this idea of governmental experimentalism remains Franklin Roosevelt.

Where Roosevelt faced a depression of the economy,
though, you face a depression of civic spirit. Where he
might use the torch of government to reignite the fires
of capitalism, you must employ the fire of democracy's
eternal ideal to light the imagination of tomorrow's
generation. This can best be done by appealing to the
innate sense in all Americans, especially the young, that
their country can be better, that it can achieve a higher
degree of contentment and security than the majority of
its citizens today enjoy. But this can only be achieved if
the people are first led to understand that they represent
a community of common interests.

Notes

1. Could demented extremists who bomb government buildings to save the nation be the direct heirs of military officers who burned Vietnamese villages in order to save them?

2. "The earth belongs always to the living generation. They may manage it then, and what proceeds from it, as they please, during their usufruct. . . . Every constitution, then, and every law, naturally expires at the end of 19 years." Letter from Thomas Jefferson to James Madison, September 6, 1789.

No. 5

Concerning the impact of the disintegration of national boundaries on national unity

A wise prince ought to adopt such a course that his citizens will always in every sort and kind of circumstance have need of the state and of him, and then he will always find them faithful

NATIONAL UNITY AND PURPOSE ARE MOST easily preserved in nations with well-established and defensible borders. There citizens have some assurance that they can regulate their affairs without the threat of intervention by neighboring states, intrusions by nondemocratic forces, or unregulated flows of immigrants.

The late twentieth century, however, has presented

new challenges to the concept of secure borders. Instant access to information, global markets, and rapid transportation—particularly when combined with motivated foreign workers and lower wage rates—have all led American industries to increase investment and production outside their own country. Capital, technology, and management, the keys to economic success, now flow freely and recognize no national boundaries. Likewise, the last quarter of this century has witnessed huge increases in the foreign share of American markets, direct foreign investment in American real estate and manufacturing, and substantial increases in legal and illegal immigration.

Immigration has always been a particularly volatile issue for nativists who are wrongly convinced that racial unity is central to social integrity. But it is also immediate and real for Americans on the margin of employment, housing, and public services who see new immigrants as a threat to their tenuous hold on existence. These and other Americans, virtually all children of immigrants themselves, must be reminded of the economic and cultural vitality contributed by previous and present-day immigrants willing to accept low-wage jobs in the hope of achieving the American living standard.

For boundaries are now transgressed less significantly by foreign armies or immigrants and more significantly by global markets, electronic currency transfers, instant communications and fast air travel. Mass culture, heavily exported by American entertainment industries, blurs distinctive taste and opinion and erodes national cultures and traditions, especially among the young. All these modern forces erode and reshape traditional democratic institutions and structures.

The United States, by virtue of fortune and geography, has been essentially an island nation. Its northern border is shared with a friendly democratic nation, Canada, and its southern border has, at least until recent tides of illegal immigration, been secured by a friendly relations with Mexico. It is forever separated by great oceans from the European homelands of its principal settlers and its more distant Asian trading partners. But those realities are eroding, and old political certainties are disappearing with them.

The new leader, in an era of change, is faced with the imperative of constantly reforming national consensus around new policies. The security of fixed boundaries, whether of the nation or the nation's mind, is now a chimera. The consensus required for governance increasingly evades leadership, and reliance on old policies designed for previous eras is a sure guarantee of disaster.

The democratic leader is now called upon to command complex technical issues, select sophisticated advisers, resist special-interest pleading, rally multipartisan consensus, and communicate complex messages to an intricate electoral mosaic. Not possessing the authoritarian implements of coercion, the modern democratic leader must depend upon his skills of persuasion and an electoral mandate that wanes more often than it waxes. The mass media, especially television, is both the source of his greatest power and the greatest threat to his authority.[1]

You will lead in a period where geographic boundaries offer little by way of security. Do not suppose these conditions will give way to stability anytime soon. The world will not allow a new leader to enjoy a predictable environment, or one favorable to national consensus, within either of our lifetimes. You will govern amid a restless, teeming global forum of which you control only part, and that only tenuously.

The old security of isolation behind artificial boundaries must now be replaced by the security of intricately interwoven global markets and shared democratic values. These now become the measure of stability and the standard for your own performance. Have you helped secure a new trade network of international trade, and have you used your power to promote the democratic alternative in emerging nations? Such actions will form the basis of your success as the world's spokesman for democracy and will determine whether you are able to unify Americans behind an agenda for national renewal.

You will either harness these changes in the national interest or be harnessed by them to the national detriment.

Note

1. The leader's power to use the electronic media to communicate with the people at large is gradually being replaced by the same media's power to diminish and then destroy him. Consideration is given in Number Twenty-Three concerning the destructiveness of the media-celebrity culture and the need for the leader to challenge the media to a higher calling.

No. 6

Further concerning the disintegration of national boundaries

It is necessary for a prince to have the people friendly, otherwise he has no security in adversity

AT THE CLOSE OF WORLD WAR II, WORLD LEAD-ers came to a central conclusion: things could never be as they were. As a result of this, they created a new international infrastructure of economic and security institutions including, among others, the United Nations, the North Atlantic Treaty Organization, the Bretton Woods conference on monetary stabilization, the World Bank and International Monetary Fund, and the General Agreement on Tariffs and Trade. Collectively this network bolstered democracy, contained communism, rebuilt Europe and parts of Asia, and supported new postcolonial nations.[1]

The bipolar Cold War order collapsed at the end of the twentieth century, however, and the 350-year-old world order based upon the nation-state is disintegrating. Sadly, current leaders have not possessed the imagination to remodel the world along similarly visionary lines. Now you must exercise the bold thinking needed to create new grand alliances. Only in a new system of international economic and political security arrangements can America enjoy the peaceful environment required to renew itself.

After the Peace of Westphalia in 1648, Europe organized itself into nation-states. Machiavelli, thought by most political historians to be the father of the nation-state, provided the intellectual framework for thinking of Italy as something greater than a mere collection of principalities. He held that common factors of history, culture, language, and religion created a common people with common interests which in turn required national leadership. The idea of nations and of nationalities, or peoples with common cultures and common interests who populated these nations, became the central organizing principle for the civilized world.

European colonial powers exported this idea of nationalism throughout the world in the sixteenth, seventeenth, and eighteenth centuries. Colonies were formed—often of vastly diverse native tribes and cults—

in the Americas, the African continent and throughout Asia. Over time, heterogeneous cultures, treated as one people by their colonial masters, came to think of themselves in this light. As colonialism began to age and then collapse in the middle of the twentieth century, the often unevenly welded cultures of these colonies demanded their own identity *as nations* in the family of nations. Empires, whether Ottoman, British, Austro-Hungarian, or Soviet, left behind nation-states or their predecessors in the wake of their demise. Thus the world came to be defined by national boundaries and nationalistic impulses, which were reinforced during the twentieth century's age of ideology. Democratic Western nations organized against German and Italian fascism, and later against Soviet communism. At stake were not only individual rights and liberties but also the integrity of national boundaries and rights of national self-determination.

As the colonial era passed, so did the age of ideology. Ideology had been a good cement against internal pressure, but when the external pressure of ideological conquest was relaxed, tribal identities, cult interests, or religious fervor exploded national boundaries into fragments. The last decade of the twentieth century saw Slovak set against Czech, Serbian against Croatian against Muslim, Georgian against Ossetian and Abkhazian, Azeri against Armenian, Russian against Ukrainian and Chechyan against Russian, Moldovan against Hungarian, Kurd against Turk, Afghan cult against Afghan cult, Hutu against Tutsi, and, throughout the Moslem crescent, Shiite against Sunni. All these and more are but the symptoms of a grander epidemic. Most importantly, these conflicts are mainly being conducted within what until recently were unifying national boundaries.

Perhaps national boundaries are simply being redrawn to reflect truer nationalism. More likely, nation-states and their boundaries are gradually giving way to tribes, cults, sects, religions and nationalities in the very narrowest sense of the word. The job requiring the greatest delicacy and discretion in the early twenty-first century will be that of the mapmaker, who must add to his skills the flexibility and imagination of the weather forecaster.

There is little of all this that a new leader can or should attempt to regulate. Many of these disintegrating forces spring from grievances predating modern memory; in some instances they must run their tragic courses. As world leader, you must assemble the stable nations—possibly through a new international peacemaking alliance with offensive military capability—to intervene where it is necessary or profitable to prevent the cancerous spread of violent local conflict. With the dramatic diffusion of lethal modern armaments, the world has become an arsenal—not a place where fires may be permitted to burn untended.[2]

This dramatic disintegration puts a greater burden on

the new leader's role as intermediary and security organizer. Be always available as a mediator, a conciliator, and, collectively with other regional powers, a guarantor of negotiated settlements. As unproductive as intervening in local calamities may seem, *laissez-faire* is not an option. History offers many bitter lessons of seemingly minor brush fires grown into conflagrations, whether the former are assassinations in Sarajevo in 1914 or "ethnic cleansing" in the same region in 1995. Gauge your involvement in regional disputes according to the following priorities: our nation's interest; the likelihood of the conflict spreading; mediation's likely success; the long-term impact of continued conflict on regional and international communities; the example to others your involvement might offer; and your ability to engage other powers as guarantors.

Volatility is natural when a world order collapses. Existing political and economic institutions are presently strong enough to prevent chaos, but stability is not self-reinforcing in a changing age. You must fill the vacuum of decayed belief with bold notions for new mechanisms and institutions designed to give structure to an emerging, as yet undefined, age.

Consider two new global organizations whose purpose would be to fill the widening vacuum created by the end of the Cold War and the increasing disintegration of the nation-state. The first—a grand alliance composed of North America, the European Union, and democratic Asia—would guarantee open markets and free trade within each bloc and among the three to prevent trade wars. It would also provide financial and technical assistance, principally through credits, loans and equity investments, to emerging democracies.

The second global institution, sponsored and supported by the new alliance, would be an international security agency. Composed of international volunteer forces under unified command, this agency's soldiers would be trained and equipped to restore and maintain peace in venues such as Bosnia, Rwanda, Somalia, and Haiti. Such post–Cold War conflicts have festered largely because of failures of will in the international community and because existing international agencies are inadequate. This new agency would be the international equivalent of NATO and would possess both offensive and defensive capabilities, making it capable—unlike current United Nations or regionally limited NATO forces—of both imposing peace and keeping it once won. To be effective a new international security force would have to have a clear mandate from participating states to undertake offensive operations to settle local and regional conflicts that threaten local civilian populations or regional stability.

These notions are intend to stimulate your own thinking in an age requiring the kind of innovation last seen at the close of the last World War. With other present leaders seemingly incapable of the bold, creative action that characterized the late 1940s, the world now calls upon you to create and empower a modern array of international economic and security agencies.

Notes

1. The genius of post–World War II leadership was not limited to heads of state. It was resplendent among deputies such as Acheson, Marshall, Monet, and Adenauer.

2. "Since none of perhaps two dozen armed conflicts now being fought all over the world involves a state on both sides we may offer an educated guess [as to what kind of new order will arise after the collapse of that based upon nation-states]. In most of Africa the entities by which the wars in question are waged resemble tribes—indeed they are tribes, or whatever is left of them under the corrosive influence of modern civilization. In parts of Asia and Latin America the best analogy may be the robber barons who infested Europe during the early modern period, or else the vast feudal organizations what warred against each other in sixteenth-century Japan. In North America and Western Europe future warmaking entities will probably resemble the Assassins, the group which, motivated by religious and allegedly supporting itself on drugs, terrorized the medieval Middle East for two centuries." *The Transformation of War*, Martin Van Creveld, 1991.

No. 7

Concerning the simultaneous emergence of nationalism in newly independent states

I also believe that he will be successful who directs his actions according to the spirit of the times, and that he whose actions do not accord with the times will not be successful

FILLING THE VACUUM LEFT BY FAILED IDEOLO-gies, nationalism will be a force both for good and for ill as the twenty-first century dawns. It must meet with strong resistance where, as in the Balkans, it is merely an excuse for violent ethnic score-settling. But it must be encouraged where, as in Ireland and Korea, it can be used to remove divisive barriers of religion and ideology. As a new leader, your strength will be judged by how seldom—not how often—you resort to force to maintain the peace. Harnessing the untamed forces of nationalism, whether through diplomacy, military power, or both, will therefore represent both your greatest opportunity and your greatest threat.

Many of these instructions are but condensed lessons of Vietnam, that painful experience that produced a wide range of often contradictory sermons.[1] But subsequent experiences have also taught us something. The defeat of the Iraqi army on the border of Kuwait in 1990 showed that a multinational military force (albeit overwhelmingly American in this case) under unified command can be effective. You must press to institutionalize such a multinational military capability in permanent form. Your immediate predecessors failed to do so out of failure of imagination, comfort with the status quo, and familiarity with traditional military institutions and alliances. The very possibility of the use of such an international peacemaking capability in venues such as Bosnia would greatly strengthen the negotiator's hand. Most importantly, you must insist—through the exercise of your own moral authority if nothing else—that European powers assume greater responsibility for both making and keeping peace within their collective spheres of influence.[2] To neglect a new viral strain of international grievances in an era of interdependence is to invite such constant turmoil that American renewal will be impossible. Restoring national unity and reforming national institutions, your central mission, depends upon a relatively stable world hospitable to democracy and legitimate national aspiration.

History is again instructive. The age of ideology followed closely upon the age of empire. As empires disintegrated, feelings of national identity began to breathe new life but were quickly crushed by political dogma and social doctrine. Now, as utopian dreams fade, long-dormant national identities emerge to fill the void of political identity and cultural aspiration.

As politics (like nature) abhors a vacuum, so power will find a focus. Men and women must have something to believe in, even if it is only a tribal identity. Belief in turn demands a prophet, and the prophet of the twenty-first century is the nationalist leader. The face of nationalism, however, need not be undemocratic. Only when a national "destiny" implies dominance does the ugly visage of fascism make its appearance.

It falls to the democratic leader to resist the new orthodoxy of national superiority both in his own country and in those that may threaten international security. The second half of the twentieth century offered the stability of a tripolar world: democratic, communist, and nonaligned. The borders of instability were marked by nuclear weapons. Proxy wars might be fought by the great powers through surrogates, but unwritten rules and unspoken limits were always observed lest conflict give way to chaos and catastrophe. Political tension provided its own stability, like opposing ropes of a great tent. The world's business was conducted under this tent for half a century.

The peaceful conclusion of the great ideological war eliminated this tension and released the national and tribal grievances of centuries. Predictably, that ancient seat of grievance, the greater Balkans, has provided an immediate venue: Serbians seek to destroy Bosnians, Armenians reopen territorial claims against Azerbaijanis, Georgians are in conflict with Ossetians and Abkhazians, Slovaks depart peacefully from Czechs, and Russian minorities are fearful in the Baltic States, Ukraine, and other former Soviet republics. Elsewhere nationalism forms its historic pyrotechnic fusion with religion, as Hindus and Moslems threaten civil war in India. Nationalism gives way to tribalism in South Africa and Angola, and in poor Somalia and Rwanda tribalism gives way to the meanest of all conflict, inter-family warfare.

Modern democracies are not immune. Reunified Germany produces neofascist nationalism directed largely against migrant workers; France witnesses the same against North African migrants. Italy experiences fractures between its wealthy north and poorer south. And the United States witnesses urban riots, led by gangs of blacks against gangs of Latinos and of both against Asian immigrants, while white suburbs feel increasingly threatened by darker inner cities. America's domestic fractures might be called mini-nationalism, for they surely manifest themselves on racial and ethnic lines.[3]

The new democratic leader is thus obliged, first, to prevent latent multicultural fractions from fragmenting his own nation and, second, to organize the international community to prevent virulent nationalism from becoming the twenty-first century's religion. As leader of the dominant global power, you will be called upon to resolve (alone or with others) a plethora of vivid nationalist and tribal grievances. Be cautious, be decisive, but most of all be discriminating. Some disputes within the limited scope of American hegemony will be within your power to resolve, as in Haiti. But be careful that, like the spirits Caliban summoned from the vasty deep, such disputes will stay resolved once our forces are withdrawn.

Seek cooperative compromise of grievances, guaranteed by several nations. Always prefer diplomacy over force. Choose skilled and loyal negotiators, but also look for the personal envoy who may have special influence. If force is required, use it reluctantly but wholeheartedly once it has been committed. Once you have unity with military commanders over the objective and are assured that it is achievable, leave strategy and tactics to those who possess the requisite military competence.[4] Do not hesitate, though, to replace those who prove to lack such competence. Also be sure that the commanders agree with you over the scope and duration of the engagement. Your principal responsibility then is to inform the people of the likely cost of the venture in human and material terms and to seek their approval. Remember Clausewitz: The army belongs to the people, and they alone can ratify its use.

Notes

1. No more controversial sermons have been recently produced than those of former defense secretary Robert McNamara, whose book *In Retrospect* represents a postmortem of a failed war. Rather than focusing on the very precise lessons to be learned from the tragic Vietnamese experience, as presented by the chastised Mr. McNamara, most attention has been focused on the degree of his culpability.

2. The distinction between peace*keeping* and peace*making* is crucial. The former is defensive, passive, and presumes a state of peace; the latter is offensive, active, and presumes a state of conflict. Peace*keeping* forces are neither equipped, trained, nor authorized to *make* peace.

3. Recall, for example, the riots in Los Angeles pitting African-American, Hispanic-American, and Korean-American communities more against each other than the dominant white majority.

4. Military theorists attribute much of the success of the Persian Gulf war to the willingness of civilian (amateur) commanders to defer to military commanders on the ground to implement strategy.

N°· 8

Concerning limitations on influencing
other states

It is necessary to be a fox to discover the snares and a lion to
terrify the wolves. . . . He who has known best how to
employ the fox has succeeded best

W ITH NUMBING SWIFTNESS, WE HAVE GONE
from a world integrated by transna-
tional ideology to one disintegrating under the subna-
tional forces of tribe and clan identity. Nation-states, the
political bricks held together by the mortar of alliance
and common interest (including common enemies),
show signs of ethnic fracture from Moscow to Tbilisi to
Mogadishu.

History's trick has been to increase America's responsibility even as it diminishes America's authority to carry it out. Cold War strategies, tactics, doctrine, and weapons are of little use in the nasty little wars carried out in back streets and refugee villages across the world.

This loss of clarity and command presents the new democratic leader of the twenty-first century with an even more formidable challenge than that of his predecessors. The great ideological war of the past half century carried its own dangers, including the ever-present threat of nuclear war; but there was also a clarity of purpose and integrity of motive that these murky times no longer offer.

The "Western" consensus, which peculiarly encompassed much of the Far East, was ennobled by its commitment to the containment of communism. The search for partnership was largely selfless. Wars were fought and young lives lost, principally by Americans, not to protect the homeland but to prevent the enslavement of others. Freedom was ransomed through the investment of blood and national treasure with little thought for conquest, empire, or even hegemony.

During this period the democratic leader had cause and moral authority to seek the participation of other nations in freedom's perpetuation. The leader rewarded friendly states with financial aid—and often with weapons of war, the principal instrument of regional influence. The leader might also deploy democracy's murkier assets, its covert intelligence and counterinsurgency forces, in the cause of stabilizing democracies, like Portugal, or friendly dictatorships, like postwar Greece and Turkey, as well as destabilizing socialist states or unfriendly dictatorships.

Now the leader faces a less pure and more mundane world, a mordant souk of local conflict, famine, epidemics, bursting populations, mass migrations, and ugly feuds. The leader must decide not only how to stir this pestilent mixture but whether he even wishes to. Presuming that he does, he is curiously less powerful in military terms than in the clearer, larger world of ideological good and evil. Nuclear weapons are virtually useless, their possible use considered laughable by tiny states and local tribes. The covert assets of intelligence forces are ironically even less effective against emerging nations who deem the obvious Western secret agent but an anachronistic curiosity. Burdened by public debt, even the leading democracy finds its grants of development assistance are slender when compared with the international demand.[1]

The new leader must venture forth into the international wilderness of mercantilist competition, nationalistic grievance, and human misery knowing that his arrows are designed for the wrong-sized game, but that his nation's future becomes more deeply enmeshed in the global thicket by the day. Isolation is not an option in the modern age. The new leader will calculate his nation's shifting advantages in trade and political influence on the margins of diplomacy, seeking short-term alliances to address transient problems. He will suffer petty slights, though, from dependent countries seeking revenge for the indignity of having accepted assistance from the superior power in more dangerous times. He will be a shackled lion whom lesser creatures taunt at a safe distance.[2]

Leadership, for the time being or until another great conflict arises, will assume the guise of restraint (in Bosnia), selective intervention (in Haiti and Somalia), and collective action (in Kuwait) in a shifting, changing world increasingly characterized by migration, competition, and nationalistic frictions. Few occasions will arise for displays of political heroism by leaders. Rewards will be for managers, not visionaries.

Great leaders shine in moments of moral clarity or historic transition. Today's light is diffuse and shifting. The new leader is more physician than knight in armor. His motto is as follows: first, do no harm.

Do not be read these words as a counsel to retreat from the world. To do so would be to prescribe a legacy of even greater troubles for your successors. They are, however, a caution against hubris and toward wisdom and discrimination. In principle your power is great; in practice it is limited. It resides primarily in your ability to persuade the people, at home and abroad, to do what is right and in their own long-term interest. But it also resides in your genius to envision new political, security, and economic structures for the twenty-first century.

Your real strength is in both the practical and the ideal. Old states and new nations will seek America's goodwill for the economic benefits involved—markets, capital investments, and financial assistance—and in the hope that the blessings of democratic stability will replace former repression and turmoil. But democracy resists imposition. Its seed may be planted from without, but the local soil and climate must be hospitable, and it must be tended locally.

You must take special care to foster institutions and structures, beyond merely commercial ones, to nourish democracy's roots in new venues. Capitalism does not guarantee democracy; democracy guarantees capitalism. Take care always to lift up the ideal of democracy—the fire that has lit the minds of men from Jefferson to Sakharov—and your influence in emerging states will be magnified.

While ideals will ignite the democratic visionary, the prospect of better food, shelter, and health will motivate the masses of men. Dostoyevsky's Grand Inquisitor thought bread to be more urgent than freedom for most people.[3] America's task, which is yours as well, is to demonstrate that the best prospect for bread lies through the door of freedom. Rampant, unregulated markets breed crime in Moscow of the 1990s as in Chicago of the 1920s. Overreaction to lawlessness and turmoil

breeds authoritarian political figures, like J. Edgar
Hoover and Augusto Pinochet, whose repressive politics
and protection of economic elites some in Russia find
tempting today.

Education of young leaders from emerging nations,
building of democracies abroad, subsidization of business training centers, establishment of career civil services—all these will win greater influence in emerging
nations than warships and grants of money. A new leader
will find innovative ways to use the lessons and ideals of
democracy as his principal instrument of diplomacy.

Notes

1. Even that relatively meager sum is presently being reduced
under isolationist pressure from Congress.

2. Americans remember with anger and dismay televised
pictures of the body of an American soldier being brutally
dragged through the streets of Mogadishu.

3. "Oh, never, never can they feed themselves without us!
In the end they will lay their freedom at our feet, and say to
us, 'Make us your slaves, but feed us.' They will understand
themselves, at last, that freedom and bread enough for all are
inconceivable together, for never, never will they be able to
share between them!" "The Grand Inquisitor," *The Brothers
Karamazov,* Fyodor Dostoyevsky.

N⁰· 9

Further concerning limitation on conditioning the behavior of other states

It will not be difficult for a wise prince to keep the minds of his citizens steadfast from first to last, when he does not fail to support and defend them

AS ECONOMIC AND SECURITY INTERDEPEN-dencies increase in the world, you will discover that your authority in conditioning the behavior of other nations to be practically and morally conditioned by America's ability to live up to its own high standards. Our greatest appeal—and therefore our strength—lies not in our threats or boasts but in our achievement, example and ideal. Authority by example increases in value because the United States, even as the dominant democracy and surviving superpower at the close of the twentieth century, possesses less ability to influence the conduct of other states by traditional economic and military means than it would appear to have. Several reasons for this may be cited.

First, naked weaponry alone may inspire fear but will never engender friendship from recalcitrant states. To encourage respect and therefore behavior conducive to the interests of the military power, superior force must be accompanied by the will to use it. Through modern media, however, the results of military action are now made instantaneously available to the world. Increasingly such strategic military targets as leadership headquarters, command and control centers, and research and production assets are located in urban areas where targeting ensures civilian casualties.[1] The death of innocents inspires public outrage as it is broadcast worldwide, and public opinion thus becomes a new element in the overall strategic equation.

Second, much well-intentioned economic assistance is not received by the intended beneficiaries. Traditional foreign aid, received mostly by Third World states, routinely falls prey to black markets and corrupt host governments. Even when this assistance made its way to the general population in such states, however, their authoritarian governments often remained isolated from any public opinion that might favor the contributing power.

Third, immune from the threat of force or the reward

of economic assistance, more prosperous states resist external influence out of national pride. In democratic states, a political leader who seeks too obviously to accommodate the interests of even a benign foreign power will be perceived as weak and insufficiently committed to his own national interest. Diplomacy based primarily on the personal friendships of leaders is ephemeral and will be swept away by national pride.

Seeing the limits of military power, of economic assistance, and of personal goodwill, the new leader will soon come to appreciate that the limit of his ability to influence the conduct of another state, benign or hostile, is formed by national self-interest. The most successful diplomatic appeals will direct themselves to the best interest of the other state insofar as it coincides with the leader's own national interest. Sometimes it is sufficient simply to persuade another state to abstain from undesired action, such as invading a neighboring state or covertly undermining its government. The powerful leader, though, will state his position unambiguously.[2] Ambiguity should be used to confuse and delay, but never allowed to encourage, a troublesome state.

Economic and military power offer more by way of perceived than real authority to those who possess them. They are, naturally, better to have than not to have, but you should not overestimate their influence on the behavior of other nations. Although weapons, force structures, and the will to use them unquestionably condition the behavior of the potential aggressor, deterrence is antiseptic rather than therapeutic. Great nations can seek to prevent others from unwanted behavior or to induce more constructive behavior. For the latter, trade and investment, the offer of expert advisers, and commercial and citizen exchanges all replace barriers with bridges.

It is in the nature of human existence that new nations, in the manner of young adults, will learn self-interest and statecraft through trial and some bitter error. Even the most well-meaning parents and friends can prevent the latter only on rare occasions. But as a new leader, you may offer benign methods in reducing the pain of experience.[3]

None would argue that example, ideal, and instruction by new established leaders to new emerging leaders are sufficient to deal with all trouble spots and troublemakers. A great nation must always have concern for its own security and the stability of the world around it. Thus you must also consider whether technology is producing military power that is usable and therefore effective, or unusable and therefore ineffective. In addition, you must examine the shape, adequacy, and purpose of the nation's elaborate security forces. If they weigh too heavily on the national purse and the national spirit, resources required to renew the nation will be inadequate and your principal mission as a new leader will fail.

Notes

1. Recall the suburban hospital in Baghdad destroyed by a "smart" bomb—with the rubble instantly telecast worldwide—during the Persian Gulf war.

2. As was reportedly done, for example, by the United States government, through its ambassador, to Saddam Hussein regarding his intentions in Kuwait prior to the Persian Gulf war.

3. "A good conscience our only sure reward" was Kennedy's perceptive characterization of the limits of gratitude toward superpower diplomacy. Inaugural address, John F. Kennedy, 1961.

Nº· 10

Concerning power that is unusable

One change always leaves the toothing for another

YOU MUST FULLY REASSESS THE VALUE OF THE national arsenal from the perspective of the actual threats to our national and collective security. That which cannot, or will not, be used is superfluous. Technology guarantees its own obsolescence and eventually makes every weapon so. Moreover, countermeasures to new sophisticated offensive weapons are almost always less costly and therefore more affordable in quantity than the weapons they are designed to defeat.[1]

In the late twentieth century, power had come to be defined almost exclusively in military, and to a lesser extent, economic terms. There was a degree of synergy to this definition. Because standing armies with their expensive modern equipment are essentially unproductive investments, only a nation capable of generating a substantial revenue beyond those required to meet ordinary civic needs could become a military power.[2] Likewise it was believed that far-flung global investment required military protection, in some cases from hostile local governments.

The Cold War generated several generations of strategic nuclear weapons powerful beyond the dreams of Zeus. These weapons came to possess a degree of automated autonomy sufficient to guarantee that even an aggressor operating under the highest conditions of surprise, stealth and treachery would himself be destroyed. Their only practical use, therefore, was to assure that no one else would use them. They were the ultimate deterrent.

But this deterrence worked only toward those countries that themselves possessed nuclear weapons, since the prospect of using these weapons against a non-nuclear power had become literally incredible. Therefore, the six nuclear powers possessed awesome force which was, except to deter each other, practically unusable.

Lesser nations took full advantage of this anomaly. Whether in Vietnam or Afghanistan, backward nations with primitive weapons defeated superpowers. As the century ended, nations with unprecedented military power became less and less inclined to use it. Exceptions were Great Britain against Argentina in the Falkland Islands and a United States–led consortium against Iraq in Kuwait, but the rule (in places such as Bosnia and Rwanda) came to be against the operation of foreign expeditionary forces.

The modern leader thus can no longer equate military capacity with deployable force. Weapons of mass destruction are not credible against those who do not possess them. Further, public opinion—shaped and reshaped by instant mass communications—has become a serious policy conditioner in democratic republics. Upon the display of casualties on television, public support often melts away. Absent a real and present threat to national security, the degree of popular support required to sustain a prolonged military operation is, at the very best, transitory.[3]

But few are the conflicts that lend themselves to permanent resolution by force alone. Ordinarily diplomacy can find some fragment of self-interest within each combatant to preempt or terminate hostilities before they run their costly course. So do not put your faith in military hardware or let our nation's destiny be held hostage to it. Contrary to the wisdom of the scientist, technology can produce military power, but it cannot tell you how, when, or whether to use it. That is a matter for political judgment when all else, namely diplomacy, fails. War is not an instrument of policy, it is a failure of policy. And weapons produced by technology are instruments of war, not instruments of policy. Our national strength is not in our arsenal but in the minds, spirits, and hearts of our people. Place your trust in them.

Notes

1. There are many illustrations of this point, perhaps none so vivid as that of the Nimitz-class nuclear aircraft carrier, the mightiest ship in human history. A Nimitz-class carrier and its complement of warplanes cost more than $5 billion. Yet this ship can be effectively disabled by a torpedo costing a few hundred thousand dollars.

2. "The history of the rise and later fall of the leading countries in the Great Power system since the advance of western Europe in the sixteenth century—that is, of nations such as Spain, the Netherlands, France, the British Empire, and currently the United States—shows a very significant correlation *over the longer term* between productive and revenue-raising capacities on the one hand and military strength on the other." *The Rise and Fall of the Great Powers,* Paul Kennedy, 1987.

3. Virtually all commentators, including military commanders, agree that the public mandate for the Persian Gulf war was transitory and could not have been sustained in the face of mounting American casualties.

Nº. 11

How a democracy structures its defenses in the modern age

A prince who does not understand the art of war . . . cannot be respected by his soldiers, nor can he rely on them

PROTECTING ITSELF AND MUCH OF THE REST of the world against the perceived threat of communism gave the United States a central organizing principle for four decades. Many lives were lost in this effort, principally in Korea and Vietnam, and much treasure spent. In the end, judging by the results, the effort was successful and therefore worthwhile—although the question will remain whether the same result might have been achieved with fewer lives lost and less-mammoth expenditures.

Success, however, brought more confusion than satisfaction. Nothing so unsettles a great power whose unity has been sustained by an external threat than to lose its principal enemy, as happened to the United States when the Soviet Union simply disappeared. What is a leader to do with an unprecedented military superstructure whose particular mission must be abandoned due to forfeiture by the opponent? There are always troubles in the world. Two questions arise: Is this military structure designed to deal with these troubles, and should it be so used?

The classic formulation is that military force should be used to protect the national interest and national security. It is thus left to the new leader to define the national interest and security and, when they are threatened, to convince and guide the people. The enlightened opinion of the people is central to the successful use of military force. One of the most dire mistakes of the Vietnam war was the persistent failure of American leadership to deal straightforwardly with the price its citizens were asked to pay.

Most simply put, national defense is the prevention of any hostile encroachment upon the nation's borders. But national defense has consistently been defined much more broadly and ideologically by America's leaders: first as the containment of communism, and now as the maintenance of world order.

Because containing communism required military,

paramilitary, and covert forces, the strength of United States foreign policy came to be equated with its willingness to maintain and use such forces. Willingness by leadership to commit American military power, even if it resulted in ineffectual or unnecessary bloodshed, came to be the hallmark of a strong foreign policy. Communism as a threat collapsed, but the definition of "strength" remained.

A host of bloody, local quarrels has broken out in the Balkans, sub-Sahara Africa and elsewhere which the United States, as the surviving superpower, is called upon to resolve. Resolving these conflicts usually requires "strength", which is to say the use of military power. Therefore the late twentieth century finds the world's leading military power caught in a trap. To be "strong" means to use military force in disputes that rarely represent any threat to United States national security.

A new leader wishing to restore meaning and sanity to the phrase *national defense,* especially as it relates to diplomacy, must first define anew the basic terms of the discussion. For example, let it be said that *defense* means the protection of the integrity and security of the borders of the homeland against any foreign threat. Let it be further said that *strength* means the ability to maintain and deploy this defense.

Having clarified with some simplicity the question of national security, there remains the issue of international

GARY HART

security, which is threatened when either one nation attacks another or when the internal disputes of one nation threaten to upset local or regional stability. Threats
to international security require response from all nations concerned. A nation's self-interest, though, cannot
be defined by another nation. The United States is in
danger of falling into yet another trap by assuming responsibility for convincing other nations that their security is threatened and, when it fails to do so, assuming
principal responsibility for restoring order. The leader of
the largest power must organize other powers to keep
the peace and convince his fellow citizens to contribute
to this cause. But he should not permit his nation to
bear the sole responsibility for global peacekeeping or
peacemaking.[1]

Your greatest power is to hold aloft, even as you
struggle toward it yourself, the democratic ideal for
those whose instincts seek it out. Those too far gone in
murderous vengeance or fantasies of national purity
must know they are not at endless liberty to dispense
their hatred and violence unchallenged by the might of
the community of stable, peaceful nations. You must establish clear conditions under which democratic nations
will act, with appropriate forewarning, against nationalist outlaws: as for example with acts of genocide, the
creation or proliferation of weapons of mass destruction, violation of the borders of a neighboring nation,
support for acts of terrorism, and so forth.

It is futile to define unacceptable behavior among nations without also preparing for its punishment. Stable democracies of the twenty-first century will be called upon to maintain quick-response, multinational, (peacemaking) intervention forces. Issues of sovereign command of sovereign forces are soluble, especially when weighed against the dangers and evils to be proscribed. These issues need not impede your efforts to negotiate the establishment of a new international security agency whose burdens would be equitably shared among members of a new Grand Alliance and whose assets would enable it to restore and maintain order in chaotic environments.[2]

Aggression unpunished is aggression sanctioned. But for every punishment also offer rewards. Peaceful nations have available a wide variety of inducements toward congenial behavior. Poverty, misery, and hunger offer the seedbed for violence. Alleviate the cause in the hope of removing the effect. People with hope are not the bandit's natural followers.

In a democracy, when the failure of diplomacy to dispel a threat requires the use of force, the consent of the people is essential before committing their army to combat. There is a beautiful logic to this notion. To obtain the peoples' consent, the imperative of the project must be explained. If it is a flawed project, the imperative cannot be explained adequately to command the support of the people. Since the people supply the army both with manpower and equipment, without their support the army cannot be moved. Therefore any proposed military endeavor must bear its own persuasive imperative.[3]

The leader must clearly estimate the cost of the undertaking in lives and money, including the costs of rehabilitating those wounded in body and spirit. With allowances for unforeseen contingencies, the likely duration of the conflict must be described, and dangers, including the possibility of failure, must be set forth. The relative reliability of allies and friends must be soberly assessed. If the principal appeal of the military venture is emotion—even the emotion of patriotism—sustained public support will be difficult to achieve.

The central military truth for a democratic leader is that the army belongs to the people.[4] This is most true under circumstances of conscription—that is, when national law requires the people to provide the manpower for the exercise of military force. In relatively popular wars, such as World War II, there is general compliance with conscription. In other wars, such as Vietnam, popular will and public support are divided or absent. When the leader in these instances knows that his effort to mount support from the people has failed, he must seriously question the wisdom of the military venture. Disengagement short of victory is one of the greatest challenges in exercise of the military arts. In the strictest sense, however, this was carried out by allied forces in the Persian Gulf war where the public offered only limited initial support, and many believe it would have been a preferable policy at several points of escalation in Vietnam.

With the disappearance of the principal identifiable threat to the security of the United States, the new leader must think completely anew about his nation's military needs and must shape its defenses accordingly. This necessarily means he must engage in the complete reform of military structures, a task never performed by a major military power absent a serious defeat. As commander-in-chief he must restructure an elaborate military system configured to confront a single ideological foe into a more slender and flexible force capable of combining with multinational forces to resolve low-intensity conflicts that represent threats to global peace.[5]

Historically, this may emerge as the greatest single task of your new leadership. No social structures are more cohesive than military ones, and rightly so. Success in combat is dependent upon unit cohesion and command and control. Such life-or-death relationships are not easily disturbed, but they can be strengthened by timely reform.

Military reform is rarely undertaken by political leaders because it presumes a degree of subtlety that few possess. But it is in the interest of the military and society at large to reform the military into a force that will be effective in the battlefield environment not of the past but of the future. To fail in this effort is to risk major military catastrophe and a final loss of confidence by the people in both their military and their political leadership.[6]

Few tasks of a national leader rise so high on the moral scale as defense of the homeland. A military establishment called upon to engage in a foreign conflict for which it is neither equipped nor trained (as in Lebanon or later in Somalia, for example) is a military that may suffer the humiliation of defeat and the destruction of its morale. A military with shattered morale is not prepared to fulfill its primary mission, defense of the homeland. As commander-in-chief, your highest duty thus is not to defend the military establishment against its critics but rather to reform it to face the new challenges of a fragmenting world characterized by low-intensity, urban violence among tribes and clans.

Reflecting on military history and the transformed threats of this new world is the best way to prepare yourself for such a complex burden.

The American military must be reformed not only to adapt to its radically altered mission but because it represents, at its current levels, an unacceptable burden on our heavily unbalanced public accounts. Military spending contributes disproportionately to our budget deficits; it drains resources important to revitalizing America's human talent; and it does not contribute to the gross national product. A secure nation encourages productivity, but so do intelligent children, good highways, healthy workers, and clean water. The question is balance, and the present demands of the military-industrial economy are out of balance.

All that has gone before is commentary upon your role as a new leader in making America the democratic exemplar to the new world of the next century. You must now consider those qualities necessary to become a new leader of national unity as the hinge of history opens on a new era.

Notes

1. Once again, the clearest contemporary instance of this point is the disintegration of Yugoslavia leading to the war in Bosnia—a war that should have elicited much greater concern and diplomatic and military response from European powers than from the United States. The European nations, which have suffered from neglect of Balkan chaos before, seem to have learned little from this painful history.

2. There is neither a military nor a constitutional barrier to American forces serving under international command, or to American commanders leading international forces. The issue is a political one, and even that stems mostly from right-wing opposition to U.S. participation in international military operations. Many of these conservative interests had little if any objection to American participation in NATO efforts to contain communism.

3. This is precisely the challenge faced by President Clinton in appealing to the Congress and the people to support his decision to send peacekeeping forces to Bosnia. It could only be done by defining America's role in the post–Cold War world.

4. The argument is from Clausewitz (see Number Seven).

5. I was instrumental in organizing the Military Reform Caucus in the early 1980s, a bicameral and bipartisan effort to educate Congress and the American people about the need and methodology for reforming our military institutions and structures. It was heavily resisted by traditional politicians and military commanders, but it found widespread support among younger military officers.

No. 12

Concerning the role of leader as exemplar
or as servant

A wise man ought always to follow the paths beaten by great
men, and to imitate those who have been supreme, so that if
his ability does not equal theirs, at least it will savor of it

THE NEW LEADER IS EXPECTED TO BE THE symbol of the nation and to represent society's highest values. Indeed, his constituents secretly desire that this leader achieve also the status of hero— that is, larger-than-life icon of society's most esteemed virtues. A nation's demand for a hero is often linked to its failure to approximate its own (sometimes heroic) standards of virtue.

This desire for the ideal contrasts sharply with

democracy's pragmatic demand that the leader also serve as a social streetsweep. Hence, society writ large desires a heroic leader, an icon, who represents the perfect type of its highest ideals; but society writ small also demands a pragmatic leader who negotiates compromises among its often paradoxical interests. These two roles are contradictory. Icon cannot be streetsweep, and streetsweep cannot be icon.

The contradiction is sometimes resolved by historical revisionism. Harry Truman, in his time as president considered the consummate streetsweep, became later in life and after his death an icon. John Kennedy, who was becoming an icon shortly before and after his assassination, has been turned into a very ineffective streetsweep by the forces of revisionism.

The last American leader to combine the art of the icon with the skill of the streetsweep, Franklin Roosevelt, did so under the circumstances of national crisis and accommodating journalism. Amid depression and world conflict, the nation desired to believe that its leader possessed superhuman qualities. The press chose to cooperate by refusing to expose Roosevelt's serious physical disabilities. Now no crisis is great enough to stimulate a distrustful public into discovering extraordinary virtues in its leadership, nor would the press forgo an opportunity to expose any weakness, failing or fault, whether or not it was pertinent to the leader's conduct of public duties.

These more skeptical times produce a lesser standard of leadership, at least for lower-order politicians. It is more important that the new leader be an effective streetsweep than a perfect icon, so long as the possibility exists for becoming, as with Truman, an icon in death. The immediate duties of the leader—preventing and punishing crime, reducing illegitimate births, waging war against drugs, balancing budgets—demand rather the skills of a national housekeeper than those of Odyssean adventurer. The difficulty, as most new leaders realize with unhappy speed, is that these housekeeping chores are intractable. They are social monsters to be wrestled with and, if fortune is kind, temporarily or partially subdued but never fully defeated. Success in the task of streetsweep being relative, its rewards are equally so.

Thus modern leadership is functional and utilitarian In contrast, classic leadership is visionary, epic, and charismatic. Citizens wonder that great leaders are so rare even as they demand that current leaders fix the potholes. Candidates for office in the United States condition public expectations by performing literally a service role—gasoline station attendant, grocery clerk, and trash hauler. If you are able to imagine Charles de Gaulle doing this, then you are able to imagine anything. Such exercises in humility, if not self-humiliation, may or may not be necessary to expiate the real and imagined sins of political representatives and temper public hostility, but they are unquestionably successful in destroying the mythology of separateness required for heroic leadership.

Before ascending the national stage the new leader must decide whether to pursue this popular course of handyman, housekeeper and servant, and thus abdicate the possibility of greatness, or steer for greater risk and glory by following a strong inner compass toward personal and national destiny. Fortune offers temporal satisfaction to the crypto-leader who aspires to nothing more than to be a handyman in the national household and a good friend to all. Such figures populate the halls of Congress and the state legislatures; they become streetsweeps in the hope of careerism's security.[1] But fortune does not favor forever the leader who sacrifices future greatness for present popularity. Familiarity and greatness seldom are found in the same person. Becoming a leader of destiny and vision is not something that you strive for, but is simply the result of who you are.

To steer toward greatness is to set your course for a lonely country. Political handymen know only envy and resentment for those who are marked for a greater destiny. If fortune has set you apart for such a role, expect for enemies all those whom fate and circumstance have cast in a more cautious mold. Different blood flows in heroic veins, and different rhythms are heard in heroic hearts.

Note

1. In the opinion of most observers of American politics, the quality of leadership declined perceptibly with the retirement of the World War II generation of elected representatives in the late 1970s. These individuals were replaced by younger, less internationalist, more ideological, and more careerist representatives.

No. 13

*Concerning that which deserves blame and
is praiseworthy in a leader*

*There is nothing more difficult to take in hand, more perilous
to conduct, or more uncertain in its success, than to take the
lead in the introduction of a new order of things*

CONSIDERATION HAS BEEN GIVEN TO THE RE-
alities that a new leader must give pragmatic attention to intractable problems of social order;
that the margin of latitude for innovation and error is
exceedingly narrow; that any perceived flaw or weakness
in the leader is magnified and exploited by critics; that
the public mood is bracketed between anxiety and
anger; and that the prospect for heroic action practically
does not exist. Still, even given the limited range for

demonstration of strong principles, a distinction can be drawn between conduct deserving blame and conduct deserving praise.

Citizens and electors are rightly exasperated by a leader who too easily capitulates to their unrealistic, paradoxical, or vacillating demands. A genuine leader is required to explain how democratic ideals can produce unexpected, unpleasant, or contradictory results. For example, free expression can include hateful speech, religious freedom may embrace socially unconventional practices and ceremonies, press liberties can produce damaging error, and public assemblies can create social disturbances.

American democracy contains abundant paradoxes.[1] Most political figures find paradox distressing and seek simplistic resolution or escape from it. But to avoid principle in doing so is to search for neutrality in a moral conflict, and moral conflict knows no neutrality. As Dante has written, there is a special place—beyond and beneath the tortures of hell—reserved for those souls who are "neither hot nor cold, but merely for themselves." Sadly, many of those elected to lead lack the courage and patience to help their constituents understand and resolve democracy's paradoxes, and therefore they seek refuge in the silence of neutrality.

Prizes are given to "leaders" who avoid contradiction and paradox by espousing simplistic methods for avoiding resolution. Praise is given to the leader who, with childlike innocence, encourages the equally childlike belief that contradictory desires are easily achievable. Thus we are told that war can be waged without bloodshed or loss of life by using "smart" weapons. Public assistance programs may be eliminated, and no deserving person will be deprived or made homeless or hungry. Public regulations are not required to prevent pollution of the natural environment. Taxes may be reduced, public deficits eliminated, and necessary public works maintained, all at the same time.[2]

Cowardice, corruption, careerism, compromise of the public trust—all are to be blamed in a leader. Most worthy of blame, however, is the leader too weak, ignorant, or childlike to insist that not all desires can be achieved without a price. As the twentieth century closes, this failure lies closest to the troubled fate of democracy in America and elsewhere. Avoidance of choice—and the absence of leadership that weighs and explains alternative courses and their respective prices, thereby demanding choice—invites history's greatest blame.

The forces of coincidence and circumstance, the forces of Fortune that intrigued Machiavelli, have conspired to muster past social commitments and have deposited all these obligations and their costs at the doorstep of our republic's progeny as the millennium closes. These commitments include public pension and medical programs; past security commitments; a large military and weapons-producing establishment; a multi-

tude of individual incentive, subsidy, and assistance programs; and interest payments required to finance the
borrowing to pay for all this.

Your response to this grim legacy will define your
leadership. From Machiavelli's Renaissance to recent
times, leaders have chosen to treat the people like children, using, in Machiavelli's case, fear and pity to "terrify
and satisfy". There are still many in American politics
who prefer to amuse and distract rather than educate
and challenge. For children, when finding it difficult to
choose, will delegate power to their elder-leader—and
thus the cynical leader, not respecting the people, main-
tains power by amusing and confusing them. Mature
adults, though, assume the responsibilities of democratic
choice if they are forced to do so by leaders they respect.
To gain respect, the leader must first respect and trust the
people. This is the modern essence of the ancient virtue
(*virtu*) Machiavelli thought was critical to the new
leader. "Fortune . . . shows her power where valor has
not prepared to resist her," he wrote, and today the valor
to resist Fortune is earned through the virtue of mutual
trust between the new leader and the people.

To govern is to choose. Not to choose is not to govern. A leader must require citizens to choose among
competing, sometimes paradoxical, public values. Leadership is easy during those rare abundant times when
public needs and desires can be achieved with available
resources. Such leadership deserves no blame, but nei-

ther does it merit special praise. The new leader will be praiseworthy if he can either limit public demand within the confines of public resources, or persuade citizens to finance their desires as they are met.

America has now achieved an age when it should not continue to debate fundamental questions: for example, the level of public assistance for those genuinely in need; the permanent level of the standing military necessary for national security; the standards and administration of the public education system; the basic standards of environmental quality for public health; and reasonable levels of taxation. Nations, like individuals, must mature. Maturity in this respect means achieving *and maintaining* agreement on fundamental public values, thus avoiding the capriciousness characteristic of adolescence.

Fundamental questions such as these require thorough debate, but they also require resolution. Constantly revisiting such basic issues breeds perpetual division and is a symptom of an immature and unsettled society. It distracts leadership attention from more pertinent and immediate challenges, guarantees constant political turmoil, and exhausts social energies better directed toward genuine concerns.

The American character, though, insists always on questioning first premises. While characterizing independence and freedom of thought, this quality can also become a barrier to resolution, action, and the progress that maturity provides. More than almost any other mature democracy, America insists upon debating and reconsidering its basic social values well into its third century, and by so doing it guarantees wider social divisions. Further, we often defiantly protect today what we were quick to condemn yesterday. Many of the most vigorous defenders of Social Security and Medicare programs are the conservative grandchildren of those who denounced them as socialist policy.[3] It is a dubious tribute to the fragility of ideology in America that programs providing benefits to large numbers of middle-class citizens are eventually discovered to possess virtues not known to exist when originally introduced by innovative reformers.

The greatest praise remains for you if you are able to guide American democracy to a new and higher level of maturity that acknowledges social and political paradox. Such leadership establishes democratic principles necessary to identify and resolve paradoxical beliefs and demands. Such leadership also helps Americans accept their often contradictory impulses in a society and world community that does not lend itself to simplistic solutions. Most of all, such leadership empowers Americans to govern themselves more maturely by choosing among competing social goods and paying for the choices.

If you achieve this extraordinary standard of leadership, you will have conquered Fortune and earned the abiding respect of your fellow citizens.

Notes

1. The best exposition of the phenomenon of paradox in America is *People of Paradox,* Michael Kammen, 1972 (winner of the Pulitzer Prize).

2. These characteristics were routinely displayed by Ronald Reagan, with "supply-side economics" producing spectacularly disastrous public deficits. Debate will continue over the question of President Reagan's conscious culpability in the long-term destructiveness of some of his policies. Some will argue that he was, according to Archelochus's definition, a "fox" who understood exactly what he was up to on many fronts; others will identify him as a "hedgehog" who had only one big idea, namely, that government was destructive. I believe him to be a classic hedgehog, but one in the Disraeli mode: "distinguished for ignorance, for he had but one idea—and that was wrong."

3. Current Republican party leaders in Congress—Senator Robert Dole, Speaker of the House Newt Gingrich, and many others—are apoplectic about government spending on domestic programs "where the people ought to look out for themselves." But none of these "leaders" would even dream of ending Social Security and Medicaid, given the overwhelming public acceptance of and dependence on these programs. Rather, they speak of "strengthening" them. There are reports that Ronald Reagan dreamed of ending Social Security, but he was quickly told to dismiss it as a nightmare.

N⁰· 14

Concerning a definition of integrity in a complex age

As the fact of becoming a prince from a private station presupposes either ability or fortune, it is clear that one or other of these two things will mitigate in some degree many difficulties. Nevertheless, he who has relied least on fortune is established the strongest

IN CONVENTIONAL DISCOURSE, INTEGRITY IS defined as honesty, and honesty as candor. Citizens of democracies rightly expect their leaders to practice honesty in the conduct of the people's business. Upon acquiring leadership in a democracy, a leader assumes a public trust. The leader is entrusted with power in the expectation it will be exercised in the public's interest rather than the interest of the leader, his friends, or his party.

So much is clear and has been part of American democratic belief and mythology since the time of George Washington. But life in general, and political life in particular, are not so simple. For example, science, technology, and the exigencies of the Cold War placed unprecedented power in the leader's hands by way of clandestine "intelligence" or secret information. Is it proper for a leader to withhold such information if it might cause public panic, as with the presence of Soviet missiles in Cuba in 1963? Is the leader's integrity compromised if he withholds secret information even from his own armed forces in the higher interest of mobilizing democracy against fascism, as Franklin Roosevelt is alleged to have done before Pearl Harbor?[1] Is it right for an incumbent leader to use surreptitiously acquired information and the intelligence assets that produced them against a rival political leader in his own country to preserve his power?

These complex questions, demanding mature judgment, rise on private integrity's border with public morality. They can be summarized thus: Is a democratic leader justified in behaving dishonestly to protect the public interest or the nation? Does the public interest ever require the leader to deceive, commit fraud, or breach the integrity mandated by the public trust? Certainly the survival of the state often requires deception and deceit; the exigencies of war can indeed reverse conventional political and personal morality. The leader who insists on candor and honesty when the nation's security requires deception cannot be said to have exercised integrity.[2]

Therefore it can be said that integrity in leaders is, under conditions threatening to the nation's security, defined by the interests of the nation rather than simply as an issue of personal morality. From this, then, the leader's exercise of integrity under such circumstances is defined as his success in preserving the integrity of the nation.

This is not an argument for fraud against the public in the normal conduct of public business. Indeed, deceit in the conduct of leadership where not absolutely required to protect the nation's integrity—whether out of desire to preserve power, to damage political opposition, or to promote narrow ideological interests—is a violation of the public trust and the leader's integrity. Certain leaders, like DeGaulle (or Stalin, who had no particular concern for either personal morality or leadership integrity) simplify this conflict by identifying the nation and its interests with themselves: *l'état, c'est moi.* The question of the leader's integrity is thus automatically resolved.[3]

But a cult of personality, even where a popular leader is concerned, is considered peculiar and probably dangerous in the modern American republic. More troublesome are instances of the confusion of power and partisanship with the national interest, such as occurred in connection with the Watergate and Iran-Contra scandals. Both involved illegal use of funds and deception of Congress and the people. Both were justified, mistakenly, as necessary to protect the nation's security. The illegal sale of arms in Iran to finance equally illegal operations against Nicaragua by the Reagan administration was primarily inspired by wrongheaded ideological pressures, while illegal break-ins, surveillance, and pay-offs by the Nixon administration were largely motivated by partisanship and the preservation of power. Neither of these events came close to a claim of right to protect, promote, or defend the national interest. Not even tenuous considerations of the nation's security could be found to justify official secrecy, surreptitiousness and deception. Absent declared states of war or national emergency, it is difficult to imagine circumstances that may justify a leader in violating the public trust.

But integrity goes beyond merely dealing honestly with the people about their collective interests. The greatest integrity is demonstrated by the new leader who is willing to challenge conventional thinking among political establishments and the public, to redefine the national interest in changing times and to propose creative, sometimes unconventional solutions. Integrity includes, in addition to the quality of honesty and the courage to challenge entrenched, outmoded power structures, the quality of being undivided and entirely whole. The undivided and whole leader is the leader willing to challenge powerful private and political interests in the interest of the nation as a whole. Thus the leader of greatest personal integrity is the leader best prepared to preserve the nation's integrity. Likewise, the leader most dedicated to the nation's integrity is the leader with the greatest personal integrity.[4]

The new leader of integrity places the national interest above power, ambition, party influence, and often popularity. Indeed, preservation of personal or party power of itself can never be a justification for behavior lacking in integrity. This rare form of integrity determined solely by the national interest surrounds the new leader with the peculiar virtue favored by fortune and history.

Your standard should ever be thus: undivided and entirely whole dedication to the promotion of the national interest above all else, and an insistence that the nation itself be always mindful of its own integrity. As with leaders, nations can sacrifice their integrity by undertaking policies at home or abroad that are fundamentally inconsistent with their character or the standards and values they have established for themselves. The leader of integrity will not permit his nation to violate its own integrity.

Notes

1. It is important to note that this charge, though frequently repeated, has never been proved.

2. Although the potential clash between a political leader's personal honor and the need to practice deception in the interests of national security might make an interesting question on a college ethics examination, it is difficult to contemplate in real life. Where the security of his nation and its people are concerned, it is literally impossible to imagine a leader who would put his own sense of honor first. Indeed, to jeopardize the security of the nation is totally dishonorable.

3. "The first to obtain fame by setting up a distinction between private and public morality was Machiavelli in the sixteenth century. He thereby fired the opening shot in a debate concerning the relationship between the two, a debate that was destined to last for centuries; and it led up to the Italian statesman Cavour saying—around 1860—that 'had we done for ourselves what we are doing for our country, what scoundrels would we be.' Thus, the rise of the state and its 'reason' is best understood as a figleaf. It allowed the notion of justice to be discarded and 'interest' to be put in its place, all without compromising the decency of individuals." *The Transformation of War,* Martin Van Creveld, 1991.

4. In the domestic arena, Ronald Reagan challenged entrenched interests, namely, the Democratic House (the Senate was Republican); was undivided and whole in his ideas; and marshaled his personal popularity to achieve great political victories. His success was due in large part to his singular determination and his detachment from conventional political bartering. Whatever he thought he was doing, however, he very nearly bankrupted the nation when his central idea, "supply-side economics," turned out to be disastrously wrong. This is not a demonstration of preserving the nation's integrity. Where the interests of the nation are concerned, intentions are secondary to results.

Nº· 15

Concerning courage and cowardice, and whether it is better to be right or popular

God is not willing to do everything, and thus take away our free will and that share of glory which belongs to us

LEADERSHIP PRESUMES MORAL AND POLITICAL courage. It is not a status granted by election but is rather a state of being. One can be elected to public office, but one does not receive qualities of leadership from the electorate; it can only provide the occasion for leadership.

To lead is to define choices and to convince a majority of citizens to adopt the choice most in the common interest. The most effective leadership is by example— that is, the leader taking a stance that is in the public in-

GARY HART

terest, even if it is unpopular at the moment. By so doing the leader demonstrates his own commitment to the common good and also encourages his fellow citizens to do likewise.

Little encouragement is required to convince a majority to pursue a course that is clearly in its best interest, but in political life the simplest case rarely occurs. Because the political leader almost always operates in a world of limited resources, choices most often arise between that which is desirable and good and some other goal that is equally desirable. In almost all cases, the best is the enemy of the good. But the best is rarely available.

The matter is further complicated because the true leader is often ahead of his time. He has insights or information not generally available to citizens or even other political leaders. This quality of vision is disconcerting to those who do not possess it. For the leader may foresee that an undertaking which seems attractive or compelling today will, in the longer view, be unproductive or even dangerous. Or he may see that a policy with little to recommend it today will have great benefit in the future. Society is rarely inclined to reward, politically or otherwise, the prophetic leader who possesses this critical faculty. He is right too soon.

Most politicians assiduously avoid the prophetic role, knowing that being right too soon is rarely helpful and often fatal to a political career. They seek instead the path of compromise and conciliation, a role that is not ignoble but which seldom offers guidance in making difficult choices or in avoiding future crises. A society intent upon preserving present gains and avoiding the disruption of existing power structures, however ineffectual, will reward the conciliator and ignore or punish the visionary.

Thus the history of democratic leadership presents a recurring cycle leading from the visionary, intuitive leader to the consolidator and conciliator. In times of crisis or confusion, democratic societies are more inclined to listen to the quaint, often immoderate voice of the prophet; in more congenial times, cautious and conventional leadership is authorized to adopt, through compromise, those elements of the prophetic message that then appear less radical.[1]

Even those who are burdened with intuitive insight seek public acceptance. They seek approval of their ideas and adoption of proposals they deem vital to the interest of the nation. Therefore even the most visionary leaders have a desire for success and know the temptation to compromise. This temptation is at odds with preserving the purity of vision. Likewise, the moderate compromiser often knows the damnation of the timid, the fear and self-loathing known to those who seek the comfort of security. The compromiser knows the satisfaction of acceptance by the established elites and the rewards of a successful career. But he will never know the satisfaction of breaking new ground,

challenging conventional wisdom, changing the boundaries of public debate, or raising the aspirations of the
people.[2]

Vision, the quality essential to charisma, is a complex
gift. It excites the people but is rarely rewarded with authority to govern. Rewards in democratic systems are
reserved for those who choose not to threaten the status
quo, or who are incapable of doing so.

Temptations toward cowardice these days have less to
do with outright deceit and dishonesty than with pan-
dering to interest groups, becoming captive of manipulative political consultants, and waging campaigns
designed only to destroy one's opposition. These and
other practices have increasingly come to characterize
political elections at the twentieth century's close. While
they are universally condemned, these practices persist
because they are effective; they produce political success
and thus reward candidates who use them. But they also
destroy public confidence in political institutions and
leaders.

Even as voters reward candidates who tell special-
interest groups what they want to hear, pay large sums to
media advisors, and campaign by ad hominem attacks
on their opponents, many more are sickened by the
cowardly, weak, and often incompetent leadership their
votes produce. The politicians elected by this demeaning
process have neither the vision to direct the nation to
a higher purpose nor the courage required to proclaim a

newer vision. In response to the startling challenges of a complex world of disintegrating nation-states and information-based economics, they offer only shop-worn shibboleths and simplistic partisan orthodoxies. The voters, offered only the lesser of this system's evils, decry their own choices or stay home and contemplate rebellion.

If you are to become a genuine *new* leader, you must break this degrading mold, first for yourself and then for others. Denounce and reject a corrupt political process, confront special-interest groups with an agenda based on the national interest, reject the contributions of their lobbyists, resist advisers whose only talent is in opposition destruction, and state your case for national renewal through the redemption of democracy's ideal.

You possess the qualities of courage and vision required to become such a leader. Fortune will decide how and where these qualities will be tested. If you have the quality of political virtue as well, then you will challenge the old order and the status quo. By so doing, you will liberate the energies of the nation to undertake a new great purpose.

Following this course, though, will bring you moments of loneliness and isolation. Conventional wisdom does not honor the prophet until it is safe to do so, usually after his death. But your reward will be the greater for having known that your own courage has inspired the nation to a restoration of greatness.

Notes

1. My own years in government, witnessing and participating in oscillations of left and right, have led me to endorse strongly Arthur Schlesinger, Jr.'s, succinct summary of American political history as swings between "periods of concern for the rights of the few and periods of concern for the wrongs of the many." The mainspring of the political cycle is largely generational and involves competing values: "Republicanism was a strain in the [American] inheritance; and the eighteenth-century dialectic between virtue and commerce, between commonwealth and property, was born again in the later dialectic between democracy and capitalism, between public purpose and private interest." After much reflection, I have come to believe America will never resolve these paradoxical values and thus is committed to a national lifetime of turbulent oscillation.

2. This is not a polemic against the normal compromise required to govern a modern democracy. It is, however, a strident polemic against those "leaders"—elected politicians of all stripes—who naturally gravitate toward the ground of least controversy under pressure from party and interest groups and by so doing forfeit any chance to elevate debate, educate constituents, break new ground, or challenge the status quo. Names could be named, but that would be to grant a significance that is undeserved; they know who they are. These compromisers are but technologists of power, seeking to preserve power at all costs. In a time of transition such as this, the true leader is a subversive with regard to existing, antique power structures.

N⁰· 16

How a leader should conduct himself to gain respect and power

Those who unexpectedly become princes are men of so much ability that they know they have to be prepared at once to hold that which fortune has thrown into their laps, and that those foundations, which others have laid before they became princes, they must lay afterwards

WE HAVE SEEN IN RECENT TIMES A VARIETY of paths followed by leaders toward respect and power. It is still the case that power and respect can be distinguished: one can have respect without power and power without respect, and it is narrowly possible for one to be a "leader" (that is to say, an elected official) with neither power nor respect except among a bare plurality of one's constituents. How then is one to gain sufficient power and respect to become a new leader in an age that grants little respect to political figures?

The respect of the people for their leaders is at a mighty low ebb. The public well of respect is nearly dry. This is so because our recent leaders have persistently shown disrespect for the people. They have deceived them in Vietnam, in Watergate, and in the events of Iran-Contra. They have refused to admit that current rates of revenue from taxes are insufficient to meet all public demands, but instead have blamed each other for public deficits and debt. They have offered simplistic formulas like "supply-side economics" for complex problems of productivity and deficits. They have demonized the poor, and they have divided the races. They have substituted worship of the market for a sense of community and social justice. And they have waged elaborate campaigns of character destruction rather than producing sound proposals for national renewal and reform.

The media have aided and abetted the destruction of respect by their preference for the entertainment afforded by partisan attacks over substantive policy debates and for amateur psychoanalysis over ideas and issues. This behavior is justified by the media's mistaken opinion that the people care only about the leader's psychological motivation (wrongly labeled "character") rather than his ideas and beliefs. Even given this focus on personalities, true leadership qualities are not treated seriously.

The qualities that consistently earn public respect and hence real political power are clarity of purpose, an appreciation of history, keenness of mind, integrity and dignity. These qualities foster and support each other. An understanding of political behavior through a knowledge of history increases the likelihood that a new leader will be clear in his purpose. A focused mind enhances an understanding of history's many lessons, and it also brings discipline to the definition of national purpose. The inner compass of integrity sharpens all these qualities, and they in turn comprise the wholeness that integrity implies. Apart from all others, the quality of dignity must be inherent. Neither wealth, power, honors, nor fame can provide dignity: for that, each leader must look within himself.

Citizens, though discouraged by repeated disappointments, angered by their leaders' disrespect for them, and nowadays inclined to shield themselves with suspicion from new claimants, still recognize the leader with these qualities, reward him with respect, and acquiesce in his use of power. Nonetheless, the new leader cannot assume that respect and the power flowing from it are immutable. The cords of trust binding leader and led are frayed, and they are liable to break if too severely tested. Therefore, even a successful leader must strengthen these bonds at every opportunity.

Disdain for leadership in today's American democracy is, as much as anything, the product of leaders' disdain for the people. Rebuilding trust in leadership can his best be done by consultation with the people at every occasion. The leader who expects to remain powerful and respected will not wait to hear the people's voice raised in anger or frustration, but will go throughout the land in search of their common sense, good judgment, and wisdom. This wise leader will also seek at every opportunity to educate the people concerning the issues that affect them. He will anticipate the coming crisis, offer preferable courses of action, and earnestly seek to persuade those in error that there is a better way. The leader who respects the judgment of the people and seeks to inform it earns constant respect himself.

Modern communications contribute to distrust by compressing ideas out of an erroneous opinion that the people cannot tolerate complex thoughts, even about their own vital business. No greater evil has been visited upon democracy than this illusory belief, nor is their a greater cause for the mounting distrust of leadership by the people. It has produced a generation of guileful leaders whose sole claim to power and respect is based upon the artifice of simplification. These same leaders, distrusting their own instincts, rely on pollsters and image consultants to tell them what to say and how to say it. Requiring neither communications director nor press consultants, Abraham Lincoln could himself debate for hours or produce the sublime Gettysburg Address. The quality of public discourse and debate and the decisions that follow from them have been severely devalued in recent years. By using overly compressed communication as a shield against complex truth, the modern leader sacrifices his integrity and therefore loses the respect of the people and the power that flows from it.

The street called respect carries traffic in both directions: to earn respect, the leader must show respect to those he would lead. No greater opportunity exists for this demonstration than in the way the leader educates the people. In a democracy, the leader has no greater responsibility than to share information he has gained in his leadership capacity with the citizens whose business he has undertaken to perform. The new leader particularly must insist that modern media serve the public that has licensed their usage instead of compressing the life from vital public discourse and trivializing public debate. By insisting on reasonable access to publicly licensed media for the purpose of educating the people and conducting the public's business, the leader shows his respect for the people, demonstrates his clarity of purpose and integrity, and thereby merits the respect of the people and the power that accompanies it.[1]

You will gain little respect by showing eagerness to satisfy every narrow private interest or by identifying yourself with each new popular cause. Strength alone attracts respect, and it is most forcefully displayed by a refusal to support those undertakings (often promoted by some demagogue) that excite the people for a time but are not in the republic's permanent interest. Always seek the chance—and there will be many—to display your independence when the popular cause does not advance the national purpose. This will demonstrate your strength of will, distinguish you from conventional politicians, and earn the respect of the people. Over time, this respect will be your greatest source of lasting power.

Even in times of disrespect for politics, there is for rare political leaders a quality known as purity of heart. Purity of heart, as the philosopher has said, means to will one thing.[2] The same theological principle may also apply to one possessing a public trust. In an age where the individual can find no breath between the vise-jaws of conservative ideology and liberal bureaucracy, one powerful human voice has been raised in the interest of humanity. It said, even under the crushing weight of totalitarianism:

I favor "anti-political politics," that is, politics not as the technology of power and manipulation, of cybernetic rule over humans or as the art of the useful, but politics as one of the ways of seeking and achieving meaningful lives, of protecting them and serving them. I favor politics as practical morality, as service to the truth, as essentially human and humanly measured care for our fellow humans. It is, I presume, an approach which, in this world, is extremely impractical and difficult to apply in daily life. Still, I know no better alternative.

Perhaps in Václav Havel's "anti-political politics" rests the secret to political purity of heart. The purity of your motives—and thus your title to respect from those you lead—is judged by the degree to which you will, in all your actions and decisions, the best interest of the nation and its people.

Notes

1. Significantly more television and radio time should be dedicated to debate and consideration of public policy issues, especially during elections, as a condition for the issuance of broadcast licenses by the national government. Limitations on campaign spending, the most important element of political reform, can only be achieved if the publicly licensed television and radio stations are required to make more time available to legitimate candidates to debate serious national issues.

Another proposed reform of political campaigning is to shorten the calendar for nominating national party candidates. Based on my own experience, this is unwise; it is yet again an effort to compress and condense, the watchwords of our age. Quick campaigns may be more efficient and less disturbing, but they are not more effective, for they virtually eliminate the possibility of an unknown (or "dark horse") candidate emerging. There is only one way to become nationally known, and that is through television. Only the wealthy candidate can afford to purchase national recognition on television. For the candidate without financial resources, only victories in early primary contests create the unpaid or free television exposure—as cruel as it is—necessary to become a national figure.

2. *Purity of Heart Is to Will One Thing*, Søren Kierkegaard. No more profound work exists concerning the dedication of energy, will, and talent to a noble cause—in Kierkegaard's case, the cause of personal salvation.

Nº 17

Defining the obligations of public service and civic duty

Where a leading citizen becomes the prince of his country, not by wickedness or any intolerable violence, but by the favor of his fellow citizens—this may be called a civil principality; nor is genius or fortune altogether necessary to attain to it, but rather a happy shrewdness

I T IS OFTEN SAID THAT THE ONLY PERMANENT duties of the democratic citizen are to pay taxes and to respond to military conscription in time of national crisis. In fact, the duties and obligations of citizenship should be in balance with its rights and opportunities. There are a thousand small ways to distinguish the true citizen and patriot from the lowly opportunist.

Sadly, today public service has become virtually synonymous with government service; government service is equated with political office; and political office is increasingly viewed as a disdainful occupation pursued only by a careerist elite. As for the notion of civic duty, there is little. Idealism in the service of country is in disrepute, tattered and abandoned after repeated political abuses of the public trust.

The new leader therefore confronts a citizenry that has resorted to the bare-bones definition of citizenship, is increasingly resistant to the tax levy, and is untested as to conscription for almost two decades. This means that the leader concerned with preserving and building the nation as the basic foundation of his responsibilities must reawaken the people's dormant sense of civic duty.

What devices does the leader have in strengthening democracy's fundamental resource? They are example, exhortation, and appeal to patriotism. Of these, the most potent and most difficult is example. For the leader to persuade his fellow citizens to place sacrifice over self-interest, collective over individual success, he must demonstrate in his own life the qualities of duty and responsibility. The times, however, do not encourage it. Instead of being seen as an act of public service and self-sacrifice, office-seeking is now seen as self-aggrandizement. Hence the appeal of the military figure, even in a society long disposed to resist the slightest scent of a dictator. Having dedicated his life to duty, honor, and country at a presumed sacrifice of personal gain, the security of his family, and the possible loss of his own life, the military commander is naturally presumed to have devotion to the national interest that is rarely believed to exist in civilian politicians.[1]

Because of the perversion of language by propaganda and commercialism, exhortation as a stimulant to idealism is debased. The power of words to move, excite, or challenge is severely proscribed in an age where advertising cleverly twists and politicians dissemble. Something very dangerous has happened when three decades after a generation of young citizens could be successfully challenged to give something back to their country, the notion of service means only a public career. John Kennedy's declaration that politics was a noble profession gave way in the 1990s to the description of Congress as a "parliament of whores".[2] The two greatest American practitioners of the spoken word, Abraham Lincoln and Franklin Roosevelt, spoke in times of great national crisis, and it may simply be impossible to rally citizens to a national cause except in such times. It may be, as some republican theorists argue, that the notion of the common good only operates as a unifying principle in times of crisis, and that in times of peace and plenty men and women only seek their private interests.

Thus concern with the survival of the nation and community remains a potent instrument—thought perhaps only in times of distress—for evoking unity needed to motivate sacrifice for the common good. We are all in this together: even unspoken, this powerful theme still promotes unity in moments of both natural and human catastrophe.[3] But more effective is the enlarged idea of the nation's future, the nation being future generations. Both are abstractions until the leader makes them real by reminding citizens that life is lived, in major part, to improve prospects for one's progeny. It is the natural ambition of all but the most callous parent to struggle for a better world for one's children—less pain and suffering, more peace and opportunity. You, the new leader, should take every opportunity to show how devotion to the common good offers the best hope for a secure and prosperous society for future generations.

In the end, the leader is powerless if the noble chords of civic duty, common good, and the interest of future generations are not heard. What then remains is not a nation but a collection of individuals occupying the same territory and isolated in their feverish drive for personal advancement, heedless of the plight of the many. In the end, civic duty, common good, and national interest are not ideas at all, but deeply felt emotions. Like courage, honor, and devotion to the human cause, these convictions can be summoned but cannot be supplied by the leader. Every man and woman must look within themselves for the noble spark, the human instinct, the core conviction that we *are* all in this together and will be judged by the nation we leave behind for future generations.

You alone cannot create a civil society where none exists. Today tribes of barbarians, both primitive and sophisticated, are at work to erode its foundations. Seek allies wherever you can—in the academy and the arts, among enlightened leaders of business and labor, in the laboratories and research centers, but most of all among those who have shown their understanding of the need to revive our national spirit. You alone cannot create a civil society, but you alone can stir the national soul to rouse the latent spark in each of us that can once again blaze as part of a patriotic flame.

Notes

1. Examples include General Colin Powell today, General Dwight Eisenhower in 1952, General Ulysses Grant in 1868, General Andrew Jackson in 1828, and General George Washington in 1788.

2. This is from the title of a popular book on current politics. Perhaps the earlier time was characterized by adolescent idealism, a beautiful theory murdered by a gang of brutal late-twentieth-century facts. If so, we should not then be surprised to find that our best young people want nothing to do with politics and government, choosing instead the material aggrandizement of the market. This matters little, of course, to those who hate the national government anyway. Apparently the idea of those who ridicule public service is that inferior leaders are a surety against effective government. There is a

certain perverse symmetry in this sentiment, and it certainly seems to be working.

3. Americans still draw together, quickly but temporarily, when some of us are hurt, such as by hurricanes in Florida, floods in Iowa, or earthquakes in California, or when our youths are in jeopardy as in the Persian Gulf war. In these circumstances, the news media play a powerful, benign role. These circumstances also suggest a coincidence between Machiavelli's theme of the power of pity and fear and my theme of national pride and unity.

Nº 18

Concerning national renewal, the church, the press, and the state

I do not believe that factions can ever be of use; rather it is certain that when the enemy comes upon you in divided cities you are quickly lost, because the weakest party will always assist the outside forces and the other will not be able to resist

ANY SERIOUS DISCUSSION OF NATIONAL RE-newal must consider two institutions singled out for protection in the First Amendment. They were considered exceptional because one concerns itself with man's spiritual beliefs, and the other with the dissemination of information in a free society. The "church" has come to be defined by the Supreme Court as virtually any organized practice of religious worship, and the "press" has come to include a vast array of electronic communications systems as well as the printed word.

A new leader concerned with national unity and renewal must give the same regard to these two powerful sets of institutions as did the nation's founders. The latter were notably concerned to keep the state from either adopting or proscribing the church, and likewise to keep the church out of the precincts of government, to a degree that seems almost quaint two centuries later. Whatever powers the church may have had over the levers of secular power scarcely survive in the late twentieth century. Indeed, it is a distinctive characteristic of these times that all institutions—the church among them—are too preoccupied with their own identity and survival to exercise undue influence on each other.

There is a sufficient current exception to this general condition, however, to observe and respect the constitutional rule of separation. Fundamentalist Christianity now seeks to promote its own culturally conservative social agenda through political channels and institutions of governance.[1] While much of this agenda is benign—strengthening traditional family structures, community cohesiveness, and so forth—other goals—proscription of abortion rights, condemnation of nontraditional families, and promotion of literalist educational standards—are distinctly illiberal and are proudly proclaimed as such. This represents a classic instance of the phenomenon so feared by James Madison: a resolute minority, not even representing the main body of the Church, seeking to impose its will on an inert majority behind such slogans as "back to basics."

Moreover, fundamentalism's methods are not always praiseworthy. The struggle is more cultural than spiritual or even political; the institutions of public education are near the heart of American democratic culture. A central goal of religious fundamentalism is to suppress all unorthodox, liberal views and antiauthoritarian sentiments. At the behest of Thomas Jefferson, among others, control of public education remains to this day in the hands of local education boards composed of citizens—usually parents—concerned with the proper management and operation of community schools. This system represents the most rugged manifestation of decentralized grass-roots democracy. The religious right seeks to penetrate these local boards in order to impose its own values on the public's education system. To mask its true intentions, quite often its candidates for local office actively conceal their true affiliations and biases.

What may seem to be relatively inconsequential in the historic scheme of things is nevertheless a timely reminder of the wisdom of the earliest amenders of the Constitution, who saw the need to protect religion from the power of the state and likewise to protect the state from the power of religion. A new leader will insist that control of education systems and policy remain with duly elected local authorities while shining an intense public spotlight on any covert effort to subvert those systems for ideological, doctrinaire, or political purposes. The highest-caliber public education system is not the property of any interest group. Establishing high scholastic standards by combining classical humanities with modern science, the leader will preempt the ideologue's call for "basics" as a mask for fundamentalism.

Even more urgent, however, is the issue of press freedom to be found in the same constitutional amendment. Those who own the presses turn all the considerable powers that pen and ink—and broadcast airwaves—can muster against any hint of regulation, even though broadcast licenses are dispensed by the elected representatives of the people, who are deemed to own them. Freedom of the press is hailed as loudly by those who operate, under public license, the electronic presses as by those who operate the privately owned print presses originally protected by the amendment.

For all practical purposes, there exists no boundary between freedom and license where journalism in the modern-day American democratic republic is concerned. Disproportionate attention has been given by the Supreme Court to issues surrounding freedom of the press. This may in part be due to the power of the press to call attention to the issue that concerns it most. A leader concerned with national unity, however, should inquire as to what mechanisms may be built into political structures to protect from their power those who do not own presses. Those knowledgeable in the law will state that recourse against abuse of press power resides in statutes and common law having to do with libel, but they also know that for public persons those protections exist in theory only. Judicial curbs on unrestrained press freedoms are seldom sought not because the press regulates itself, but because the cost of litigation and the impossible burdens of proof add yet greater protections to those of the Constitution.

Those looking back from the future will have cause to remark on the unrestrained and un-self-regulated license of the modern press and its power to intimidate political leadership. The new leader will not be master of his office or his soul if he succumbs to this intimidation.

Rather than seeking terms of easy friendship, a prudent leader will maintain respectful separation from those who have their own commercial interest in judging his performance. But a new leader will, through patriotic appeal to the national interest, enlist leaders of both the religious and journalistic communities in a search for national unity where forces of division from within or a threat from without require it, and where neither of them seek the instruments of power for their own purposes.

Note

1. This is particularly true today regarding claims by right-wing religious interests on the Republican party in terms of their own social agendas and their right to influence the selection of its national leadership.

No. 19

Concerning a leader's response to
organized pressure and particular interests

*Everyone sees what you appear to be, few really know what
you are*

THERE WAS MUCH DISCUSSION AMONG THE
founders of American democracy con-
cerning the formation of "factions," or what today are
called special interests. These founders, who possessed a
transcendent sense of the national interest, believed the
new nation would rise or fall on the willingness of its
citizens to set aside their individual and group interests
in favor of the commonweal when the national interest
required it. The founders knew that factions were inevitable, but they also believed they would balance each

other in a political harmony of interests, a national choir of voices that prevented any group or collection of groups from achieving predominance. There being no excessively powerful factions, strong executive leadership was not required to tame them.

But now, narrow interests have occupied the two traditional political parties. They dictate policy, finance campaigns, control legislative initiatives, inhabit the halls of power in Congress and the White House, and determine who will or will not be a candidate for national leadership. Public frustration with these two closed systems may lead to the formation of a third political force by the end of the century.

In the middle of the twentieth century, efforts were made by an activist national government to address the needs of particular regions, with programs such as the Tennessee Valley Authority; of urban areas, with transportation and human relief programs; of communities, with a range of special programs; and of individual groups, such as farmers, nurses, teachers, retired persons, and virtually all other sectors of society. Soon it became apparent that largesse from a national government, growing in response to world wars and domestic needs, was best secured by organized pressure. Every element of society therefore organized its members to demand relief or assistance. So long as an expanding economy produced an expanding national treasury, Congresses and presidents made every effort to respond to these pressures on the evident theory that national well-being was produced by the increased well-being of the expanding multitude of factions.

This theory is true only insofar as the feeding of factions at the national trough does not come at the expense of the national interest, and insofar as the members of factions do not lose sight of this transcendent national interest in pursuit of their own. Sadly, as is evidenced by annual deficits and the soaring national debt, both these failings have occurred. This has come about as much as anything because of the failure of real leadership. Thus the new leader must assume a heavy but historic burden.

The new leader must reclaim the national interest. He must identify, define, explain, and insist upon it—for if he does not do so, no one else will. The new leader is obliged to hold up the standard of the national interest and gauge all factional initiatives against it. The new leader must also be steward of the national treasury. Every demand cannot be met, however meritorious; even a great and powerful nation like ours possesses finite resources. The highest priority must be given to those undertakings that contribute to the definable goals of the national interest.

"Politics" is the epithet given by average citizens to the routine activities of those elected to govern, and it is usually meant to describe the effort made by elected officials to satisfy the demands of special-interest constituencies. In ordinary times, when the republic is at ease, this conduct may be casually sanctioned. But, today, when distress and anger is widespread, the parties offer little to the leader, since they themselves have become mere factions or coalitions of factions. Thus it is left to a new leader to erect a noble standard.

The new leader is required to stand alone. To offset the collective power of special interests, you must become precisely the strong defender of society and the nation not envisioned by the founders. You must set yourself apart from established political structures that have become useful at organizing power-sharing arrangements and little else. Indeed, the more you are seen as the product of a disfavored political system, the less authority you can command to raise the nation's standard.

The new leader's power thus must come directly from the people. You must challenge the people at large to set aside narrow factional interests for the sake of future generations. You must force them to confront the stark choice between consumption for the immediate gratification of the few versus long-term investment in the well-being of the many. Gratification—defined as unnecessary consumption—must be deferred, perhaps for a generation or more, until the nation regains fiscal stability. You will receive a mandate to govern only by espousing a specific platform for reform of tax, education, health and welfare, and military institutions and structures and identifying a vote for you with a vote for this platform.

If you derive your power directly from the electorate, bypassing the established political structures and refusing to bargain away your independence in exchange for brokered power, you will walk a road that is more perilous and lonely but which leads to greater glory for the nation and yourself. Your strength will derive from your insistence upon the nation's interest and your use of it as the measure of all projects. Your opponents can only attack you yourself, because their base in special-interest politics is patently inferior in the eyes of the people.

By this method, the new leader drives a wedge between the people and those leaders who have organized them into factions. Unable or unwilling to serve the larger end of national renewal, these politicians derive their power from procuring a portion of the nation's resources for the few in their faction. As a new leader you must require the people to choose between their role as members of a civil society and their role as members of factions and interest groups. If you choose the traditional role of organizer of coalitions and broker of shifting political arrangements, you lose your stature as a leader above leaders. As a new leader, you must trust in the people themselves to choose the nobler course.

Nº. 20

Concerning liberality and meanness

He should endeavor to show in his actions greatness, courage, gravity, and fortitude

A LEADER IS CALLED UPON TO EXERCISE POWER in ways which, in the case of military action, may lead to the loss of life; in the case of distribution of largesse, may cause distress in those not favored; in the case of pardon, may not grant release; and in the case of granting favors, may leave party and friends angry and unsatisfied. A democratic leader must, above all else, choose. The choice is rarely between good and evil; it is more often between two goods—or between two evils.

Defining the terms of a debate is one of leadership's

neglected powers. When most creative or clever, a leader will frame his own choices or at least condition the manner in which his choices are presented to him. A leader is most successful when he is able to force his opponents to accept his terms in framing a choice. In many cases, however, the choices will be framed by competing interests or other contradictory forces and forced upon a leader by circumstance and fortune. Many choices have to do with granting or denying favors; for every favor granted, the leader has for enemies all who were denied. It is a fundamental principle of leadership that all cannot be satisfied. Whether the leader or others have determined the choices, however, the spirit in which his decisions are made will say much about his greatness. A democratic leader will seek to show in everything he does a fundamental liberality of spirit.

Here as elsewhere, I disagree with Machiavelli, who held that "a prince should guard himself, above all things, against being despised and hated; and liberality leads you to both." He advised an autocratic leader on the art of wresting power from crown and church in the interest of creating a national republic. Here I try to advise you on the art of renewing and uniting a mature democratic republic that will tolerate meanness and deception against its own people only so long as it takes to uncover them, which these days is not long. To treat the American people meanly and deceitfully is to invite their equivalent response to you.

What is needed instead is a new understanding of liberality in an increasingly illiberal age. Today it has come to mean merely the inclination to use instruments of government to achieve equality of opportunity, if not also of status. But the idea of liberality also connotes the freedom of individuals to express themselves as they choose, openmindedness toward democratic reform, generosity not only of purse but of spirit, and tolerance of those of different background or opinion. These qualities in a leader are rare and highly prized.

Leadership requires strength, determination, and the willingness to say no to both friends and opponents in the interest of all. The question is *how* this will be done. It can be done meanly, in which case the leader angers not only those whom he has denied but also those whom he has favored.

If liberality denotes a largeness of spirit, meanness denotes a smallness of spirit. For the qualities of liberality and meanness have little to do with the ideology of the leader, they have to do with the spirit of the leader. As an excess of liberality produces profligacy, so an excess of conservation produces meanness. In both cases, excess undermines authority. Few now quarrel with the conclusion that perceived profligacy by Democrats in the 1960s and 1970s led to Republican penuriousness in the 1980s and 1990s. The net effect on the people of these lurches left and right is to question the ability of either party to govern with both compassion and efficiency.

139

An imperfect policy undertaken with liberality is often preferable to a favored one undertaken meanly. This is because the manner in which a nation seeks to achieve its objectives affects the feelings of the people toward their leader and toward themselves. A leader characterized by meanness surrounds himself by mean-spirited assistants and will soon find himself surrounded by a mean-spirited nation. It is possible to govern a great nation meanly, but it will very soon no longer be a great nation.

Meanness in the leader is manifested in demonstrations of vengeance toward opponents, vindictiveness toward dissenters, narrowness toward the disfavored, intolerance toward those who disagree, and incapacity to think anew. Because he is subject to the limitations of all humanity, the successful leader will know bitter defeat, anger at his opposition, and the fear of failure. Although liberality is not superhuman, it does reside in a dimension beyond the usual political emotions. The truly liberal leader instinctively knows the potential greatness of the nation and will summon, as Abraham Lincoln did, "the better angels of our nature."

Sclerotic ideologies have given meanness new life and chained the instincts of liberality. Modern liberalism itself has become, by virtue of its exclusivity and self-satisfaction, illiberal. Conservatism, once the fountain of authentic liberalism, has become mean, smug, self-satisfied and fearful of liberality.[1] The new leader therefore must reawaken latent liberality within the people and not hope to operate successfully within political structures characterized by meanness.

Much of this discussion is intended to encourage you to restore historic content to liberalism. As used in current discourse, the term has become synonymous with compassion at best, and with profligacy at worst. Instead it was meant to describe a frame of mind connoting resistance to dogmatism, authority, and narrow-mindedness. Modern-day conservative opponents criticize liberalism's sometimes casual sympathy and—based on a philosophy of interest, not compassion—insist upon a more traditional definition of justice. While current liberalism broadens justice to mean equity, conservatism understands justice to mean the process or act of determining right from wrong, regardless of mercy or compassion. Through your arguments and actions, you must demonstrate that open-mindedness need not threaten traditional values, that generosity is possible without wasting public resources, and that justice can have both a legal and social face.

As a new leader you will find most ideological quarrels unwholesome and unrewarding. Avoid them as much as possible, for they will drain energy from more productive pursuits. But you will do much to elevate public dialogue if you rescue these important words from current political black markets and restore their integrity and value. Liberalism can be compassionate without being spendthrift, even as it resists old authoritarian orthodoxies. And conservatism can insist on justice in a literal sense without being mean, even as it protects our cultural heritage.

There is courage in liberality, especially in an illiberal age. It requires courage to confront mean-spirited forces and offer hope for a more tolerant course. The refusal of a new leader to counter meanness with meanness may make him seem irresolute and weak. Thus courage is required, and dignity too, to reject the temptations of revenge, duplicity, and narrowness. The more magnanimous the leader, the more he is set apart in an age of meanness, and to be set apart can often be dangerous. To be set apart is to be different, and difference is always suspect.

Liberality in an age of meanness demands leadership that trusts the better instincts of the people. Meanness in leadership appeals to baser instincts, such as fear, anger, and intolerance. These are present in all men, but so are charity, goodness, tolerance, and respect for the human community. The leader chooses which values and instincts to tap—and by his choice, he demonstrates those qualities himself. If he chooses fear, anger, and intolerance, he adopts meanness as his course. A leader may govern, at least for a time, from this base; however, having sown the wind, he will reap the whirlwind. Intolerant, mean-spirited people soon become an intolerant, mean-spirited nation, first angry at their neighbors, then at themselves.

By trusting the better instincts of the people, the leader adopts liberality as his course. He demonstrates his confidence in his fellow citizens, exhibits the courage to challenge the forces of meanness and intolerance, and erects a higher standard for himself and the nation. The leader characterized by liberality will hold the people to a higher standard, forcing public debate to a higher, more instructive level. He will strengthen the foundations of civil society. Most of all, he will make participation in public affairs and the life of society attractive to young people, the next leaders, and awaken the idealism of future generations.

This is the greatest legacy of the leader known for liberality of spirit, and it is this legacy that you should seek to build. Reject intolerance, narrowness, and meanness, but also resist profligacy and irresponsibility with the public purse; none of these has to do with liberality. Demonstrate an expansive spirit and a great soul. Exhibit tolerance for all but the intolerant, generosity toward all but the mean, liberality toward all but the illiberal. Most of all, liberate liberality from liberalism. Then you will be a genuine new leader.

Note

1. The poet W. B. Yeats made this point more artfully: "The best lack all conviction, while the worst are full of passionate intensity."

Nº. 21

*How certain leaders lose power
and influence*

*He ought rather to discourage everyone from offering advice
unless he asks it*

O F THE SEVERAL WAYS A LEADER MAY LOSE power, the most usual are these: clinging to office too long, loss of conviction, and breach of the public trust. All represent rarely forgiven forms of betrayal, but the last is the least forgivable.

Careerism is the disease that afflicts those who suppose their own political success to be necessary to the public interest. Each attempt to lead is an act of arrogation, salvation from which is to be found only in the distance that humility creates between public service and personal ambition. Only the greatest leader is indispensable, and even then only for a time; a true leader knows his opportunity for greatness is fortune's gift and not his by divine right. There is a grace in leaving power that marks a true leader even more than the manner of obtaining it. The lack of this grace is the careerist's stigma. The careerist may cling to office, but he will not forever cling to power and will almost never earn respect.

Familiarity with office may also erode conviction, causing a loss of the mission and purpose that characterize the new leader. The patriotic citizen assumes the burdens of public service and leadership out of a duty to enhance the commonwealth. Power provides this opportunity, but too often it becomes an end in itself. When this occurs, conviction is lost, and idealism gives way to cynicism. Then power as an instrument for contribution to the well-being of the nation becomes merely power's desire for itself. The people soon recognize the leader who seeks power simply to fill the vacuum in his own soul.

The brother of the leader without conviction is the one who has lost courage. Seldom is a leader chosen who does not possess a degree of either or both. But just as time brings wisdom to a few, the currents of time wear down conviction and courage in the many. The desire to hold on to office and power—careerism—encourages temporizing, accommodation, and compromise instead of strength, independence, and integrity.

Acts of raw courage by leaders are known to be rare, for they almost always require action against self-interest. Though longed for by the people, when a courageous leader does appear most often he is punished. The cautious leader, the one who waits until consensus forms and whose own light flickers dimly, receives the reward—but not forever. The time comes when the people tire of careerist accommodation, caution, and lack of conviction. Power and influence are finally withdrawn from the leader who is prepared to sacrifice everything to keep them. Rarely, though, is the courageous leader rewarded for insisting that the nation face an unpleasant truth. When this does occur, it is often after power and influence have been lost and he has been rejected.

In an age notably lacking in conviction and courage, faithfulness to the public trust is meanly gauged. However low the standard, though, it is a standard nonetheless. It can be breached in countless ways, including political corruption, personal corruption, favoritism to friends and party, abuse of power, or dereliction of duty. To seek and accept leadership in a democracy is to assume a public trust, a solemn commitment to place the people's interest above all else. What is right for the nation? What is in the people's interest? These are the questions the leader must ask. They are questions of will and intention more than performance and achievement. The leader whose sole concern is the commonwealth and the duty of trust he owes to it, even though he commits errors in carrying out his office, will retain the confidence of the people and the power that confidence grants.

But where the leader loses confidence and trust in the people, as demonstrated by resort to manipulative campaign techniques and favoritism to special interests, before long they will lose confidence and trust in him. Consider the fall of Richard Nixon. Beguiled by power, seduced by sycophants, and uncertain of his presence even in his own skin, he permitted sour vengeance to replace keen judgment. How little power suffices to cure the want of personal security and lack of self-confidence in a leader. Whenever the power of leadership is sought to fill this want, it has produced disaster and defeat. There is not enough power in the world to fill the awesome chasm of megalomania. Not having confidence in himself, Nixon found it impossible to have sufficient confidence in the people to deal directly with them.

Power is not only lost through misuse, but also lost through nonuse. It is surprisingly common for a political figure to pursue the grail of utmost power only to discover, having got it, that he does not know how or when to use it. That a leader should be timid in the exercise of power is occasion for surprise, but it is the mark of uncertainty and weakness. Faced, as is often the case, with distasteful alternatives, the politician often seeks to avoid decision, but finally he must choose between those same alternatives or exercise his talent to create new ones. As always, it is desirable not to let fortune frame your choices. Our teacher Machiavelli has suggested that leadership virtue is the ability to use and even cause emergencies to help create new choices. Some say William Randolph Hearst did this with the *Maine;* some say Woodrow Wilson did this with the *Lusitania;* some say Franklin Roosevelt did this with Pearl Harbor; and some say Lyndon Johnson did this with the Gulf of Tonkin. Whether these claims are true or not, neither wise counsel, your own integrity, nor political morality can advocate that you look for ships to sink in order to demonstrate this virtue. The options you create by such actions are usually as unpalatable as those that fortune presents you.

The final test of leadership is courage in the exercise of power. Reluctance to use power—desire for the easy and the popular course—is the people's invitation to search for a new courageous leader.

You will hold and increase your power by not needing it. You will increase your influence by employing it only to advance the public's interest. Be comfortable with your own soul, and you will be comfortable with power. The great leader does not need power to become whole or to give his life meaning. His greatest satisfaction is to promote the commonwealth and to serve the people's good, and he seeks power only to that end.

N^{O.} 22

Concerning the personal assistants of leaders

The first opinion which one forms of a prince, and of his understanding, is by observing the men he has around him; and when they are capable and faithful he may always be considered wise, because he has known how to recognize the capable and to keep them faithful

ONE OF THE GREATEST BUT LEAST UTILIZED tests of a leader's wisdom and prudence is the quality of those with whom he chooses to surround himself. Clearly, those entrusted with the leader's confidence and permitted to share and dispense his power must exhibit loyalty and faithfulness. The leader must know that those in whom he places his trust will wisely advise him, faithfully execute his wishes, and diligently carry out his policies.

The most reliable seconds are those whom he has known and with whom he has been longest associated. Time fosters trust. Time also fosters unspoken communication among leader and assistants. Assistants who have traveled many miles with the leader, knowing his methods, will find themselves able to sense his wishes in anticipation of command. Even in a subordinate role, they will "speak for" the leader, knowing how *he* would have spoken.

Those familiar with the leader and his seconds will also come to know those who faithfully represent his views and ideas. Those so entrusted will gain power from the trust they have earned from the leader's followers and the people at large. The leader's trust in these assistants will be magnified by the people's trust in them as reliable representatives of the leader himself. Such authority cannot be conferred by symbolic anointment, even by the leader himself. It must be earned over time.

More important, however, is the window his assistants afford into the nature and qualities of the leader himself. Assistants represent the leader both literally and symbolically. The leader who lacks confidence surrounds himself with weak and unimpressive seconds, for he is afraid of being overshadowed by strong and accomplished figures. The strong leader will seek out the most talented and capable assistants, knowing that their success will cause the people to respect him for his own strength. The leader confident enough to surround himself with the best assistants is a leader afraid of little. Of such a kind was John Kennedy, who elevated to public office individuals of proven merit, energy, and intelligence—though some showed less than wisdom on policies such as Vietnam. Few presidents since have demonstrated the confidence or magnetism necessary to attract an equal caliber of advisers.

In time, the qualities of the leader come to be reflected in the assistants, and those of the assistants in the leader. Assistants must be honest, purposeful, and dedicated. These qualities ensure that the leader will himself be seen to have them. Honest assistants will not long serve a dishonest leader, and an honest leader will not surround himself with dishonest seconds. Over time, the qualities of both cannot significantly vary.[1]

The leader's assistants must not be more ambitious for themselves than is the leader for himself.[2] It is not uncommon for assistants to assume the subordinate role as a means of furthering their own ambitions. Knowing they may not possess the leader's qualities, such assistants use his authority to pursue their own interests and causes. This is particularly true of the new assistant, the one not tested by time. The leader must beware of such tendencies, for in such circumstances the people do not understand whether the willful assistant speaks for himself or for the leader. Therefore it is a central tenet of leadership that assistants accept the principles and policies of the leader and serve only to achieve them. If a leader is unable to curb the ambitions of his assistants, he is unable to lead.[3]

The final and most critical quality in an assistant is loyalty. This quality is in short supply in politics today. Assistants are more eager to have the good favor of journalists and lobbyists than of the leader. Privileged information is exchanged for favorable notice, and the friendship of the media is deemed more important that the continued confidence of the leader. These are the signs of a faithless age and represent a political disease of epidemic proportion. A leader unable to command the loyalty of his assistants will not long command the loyalty of the people.

Therefore it is imperative that the leader brook no disloyalty. To do so is a sign of weakness. Disloyalty in assistants is the greatest sin and corrodes the leader's authority more certainly than attacks from the opposition. An example must be made of disloyal assistants so that all will know the leader rules his own house and will not be mocked. (As Voltaire said of the British, they hang an admiral occasionally to encourage the others.)

Disloyalty is a form of personal treason. The honorable assistant, finding himself in unalterable dissent from the leader over principle or policy, resigns in protest if necessary.[4] The disloyal aide keeps his position of trust but betrays the leader by elliptical and surreptitious dissent; he remains in the inner council but betrays its secret deliberations. This practice is the coin of the realm in our nation's capital, and it is symptomatic of a greater cancer spread throughout the body politic. It is the cancer of careerism, ego, and self-importance. This cancer mounts a deadly attack on the national interest and finally discredits patriotism itself. Like a political Gresham's law, disloyalty debases the sound currency of loyalty and trust.

The quality of genuine loyalty is superior to all others. But loyalty in politics is best characterized as Oscar Wilde once characterized truth: it is never pure and rarely simple. For the political assistant bears two bonds of loyalty, one to the leader whom he serves and the other to the public interest. Too often in recent years—most notably in Watergate, but also in Iran-Contra, Vietnam, and other catastrophes—these two loyalties have come into conflict. Too seldom have assistants caught in such a racking dilemma sought the honorable course.

As a new leader, you will insist that those who assist and advise you owe their highest duty to the nation. You will rightly counsel them to bring any conflict they find between your policies or actions and the interest of the nation directly to you. If you are unable to convince them of the rightness of your policies, or they fail to convince you of their error, then you must encourage them to resign—quietly if they wish you well, more openly if they wish to call attention to the issue. Either path, if carried out with dignity and respect for you and the nation, reflects a kind of higher loyalty. The more you are guided by such purity of heart, willing only the best interest of the nation, the less you will be taxed with this dilemma.

The leader who is confident of the loyalty of his assistants is thereby liberated to govern with wisdom, prudence and strength. Many will judge you by the talent and ability of those who assist and advise you. Even more will they note with disfavor if you tolerate inferior or disloyal aides. Either failure is cause for reproach.

Nothing will mark your own service or character more than your power to attract accomplished persons of integrity and loyalty to share the burdens of leadership and national service.

Notes

1. Ronald Reagan's assistants mirrored his ideological inflexibility, Richard Nixon's his vindictive partisanship, Lyndon Johnson's his suspicious cunning, and Jimmy Carter's his provincial moralism.

2. "But to enable a prince to form an opinion of his servant there is one test which never fails; when you see the servant thinking more of his own interests than of yours, and seeking inwardly his own profit in everything, such a man will never make a good servant, nor will you ever be able to trust him; because he who has the state of another in his hands ought never to think of himself, but always of

the prince, and never pay any attention to matters in which the prince is not concerned." *The Prince,* Niccolò Machiavelli.

3. Though not willful for himself, the most obvious recent example of the deputy operating on his own came after the assassination attempt on President Reagan, when Secretary of State Alexander Haig declared that he was "in charge" of the government and "the vicar of policy" at the White House. In most instances, the self-promoting assistant operates anonymously as a "high-level source" or "White House staff member" currying favor with the press.

4. Such personal honor was displayed by former Secretary of State Cyrus Vance in resigning from the Carter administration over the issue of the failed hostage rescue mission in Iran in 1980, as well as by Ambassador Warren Zimmerman (among others) in resigning over the failure of America to respond to atrocities in Bosnia in the 1990s.

Nº 23

That one should foster the media's higher responsibilities by resisting its excesses

Nothing can be so uncertain or unstable as fame or power not founded on its own strength

THE PRESS IS THE ONLY INSTITUTION, SAVE for the church, singled out for special protection by the Constitution. This First Amendment passport, however, represents a two-way street. The press is specially safeguarded against state censorship, restriction, or prior restraint; in return, its privileged status represents a public trust. The press is therefore under constant obligation to prove worthy of this public trust by providing accurate, fair, and balanced attention to the public's business, by demonstrating a high degree of maturity and responsibility, and by restraining its more partisan and sensational instincts. Today this public trust is honored only in its breach.

Thomas Jefferson is recalled to have judged that, if required to choose between a free government and a free press, he would choose a free press. He would have cause to reconsider this relatively youthful opinion later in life. A more contemporary commentator would say, with greater pungency, that there is a free press in America for everyone who owns one. Here, in two remarks, is the dilemma of the press in modern democracy: its importance as critic of government, and the increasing concentration and extension of its own power. The new leader is obliged to consider both.

Several recent developments have compounded the complex role of the press in modern society. First, "the press" has come to include electronic as well as print journalism and has thus come to be known generically as "the media." Second, journalism generally and political journalism in particular now primarily serve competitive commercial purposes. Third, ownership and management of the media are being concentrated in fewer hands—and in the hands of those for whom the communication of information is subordinate to the production of entertainment and amusement.

In addition to all this, the media's performance is transient. One story or personality replaces another on an hourly basis. Leaders' reputation, the foundation of respect, are under constant assault by media "character scrutiny." Their ability to sustain public focus on enduring, systemic public problems like budget deficits, urban decay, or military reforms is made almost impossible. Sustained public attention being crucial to creating leadership *authority*, it is little wonder that lasting solutions to intransigent problems become almost impossible.

A new leader is required to step into these potent whirlpools by virtue of his need to communicate information and ideas and answer his critics concerning public issues of the day. The leader is obliged to seek every legitimate means to communicate ideas, policies and proposals regarding the public's business. He must do so in ways that do not simplify or dilute the information or "message" he seeks to disseminate. He must exercise candor and take precautions to prevent distortion of the ideas he wishes his constituents to hear. This task is compounded, however, by increasing media attention to the leader himself.

Every pressure is brought to bear in the media age to force the leader into the category of celebrity. Celebrity is the condition of being celebrated or held up for public notice or attention—sometimes for some achievement or deed, sometimes for sensation, sometimes for little reason at all. In recent times the political figure is seen more and more as a member of the celebrity pool.[1] Politicians now gladly accept the vaudevillian's abuse by becoming entertainers, displaying "human" qualities in the hope of enjoying the entertainer's fame. The effect of celebrity is diminished stature: "When the world was young and there were men like gods, no reporters were present . . . only poets."[2] In an indiscriminate celebrity culture, either all are heroes or all are fools.

To avoid the distractions of celebrity and direct attention instead to public business of real consequence, the new leader must judiciously avoid the spotlight of publicity that sweeps widely and erratically through the groves of public leadership. Celebrity is ephemeral and shallow, its Faustian bargain trades dignity for fleeting fame. Celebrity does not abide. It reflects no genuine value—neither that of legitimate fame for great deeds nor the infamy of great misdeeds. Forces that seek to reduce the serious leader to a celebrity are conspiring in the ultimate destruction of the leader and of politics itself.

The task of communicating with the electorate while escaping celebrity's distractions is increasingly problematic, though, since the same media are the arena for both. This is the great danger of losing the distinction between the media as entertainer and as informer. The new leader must cut with one edge of this sword without being cut by the other. The wisest counsel would advise that you refrain from crossing swords with the press; but a leader who cowers in fear from those who elect themselves his judges will soon lose the trust of the people.

You must make an extraordinary effort to focus attention on public business and not be distracted by the clamor for amusement and celebrity. This clamor represents the most serious threat to the possibility of leadership in our nation today; there is about it some undefined, irrational struggle for power, or at least for the disintegration of power. It can be suggested, for example, that the ugly and unprofitable attention now given to the British monarchy is not merely a reflection of the media's often mindless commercialism. Underlying it is also a theme of anger and contempt for this form of traditional authority. Who is to say, if this anger succeeds in destroying the British monarchy, that it might not just as easily be turned to the destruction of authority in the American republic?

Since Watergate, there has been a perceptible increase in the media's arrogation to itself of the role of tribune of the people. Over the life of the republic, the media have gone from watchdog to critic, investigator, and tribune. Originally, in classic Roman republicanism the tribunal was a democratizing force, representing the people against monarch and nobles. But as its power grew, it soon became its own form of tyranny, attacking and eventually contributing to the destruction of the republic. The Roman tribunes became dangerous demagogues, causing leaders and citizens to fear the "self-elected tribunes of the people." Through tabloidization and sensationalizing of politics, the media—the modern self-elected tribunes of the people—are close to becoming equally dangerous demagogues. They undermine authority and discredit leadership by holding it up for contempt.

When political leaders and the media are both held in contempt by the people, as much as anything because of their mutual and growing blood feud, how can either emerge with dignity or authority? In recent years politicians have refrained from responding to media attacks, fearing the proverbial fight with a man who buys ink by the barrel. But increasingly politicians are fighting back, pointing fingers at their accusers and raising the intensity of the shouting match. Though it is important for duly elected officials to protect and preserve the mandate granted by the voters, the net effect of this confrontation is to discredit both the media and politics.

As a new leader, you must avoid engagement in a debate with the media concerning its proper role in society. This is a debate you cannot win and should not join; it is for the media, exercising whatever degree of self-control they can, to gauge and limit their own role. In doing so they should avoid the temptation to hide behind the First Amendment. The media's avoidance of self-criticism is too often excused on the ground that it invites limitation of their special constitutional privileges. No one, however, is seriously suggesting state restrictions on press freedom.

Your abdication from this debate, though, must not

be viewed as weakness. You will be criticized as much as you deserve and undoubtedly more so. You must accept even criticism that is unfair; but do not capitulate or accept undue blame in an effort to curry favor with the media or the people. There will be more than enough to apologize for, simply because you are human; let your conscience guide you, and you will proceed wisely.

Free and responsible media are crucial to public debate. The media demonstrate the loudest concern over the issue of state censorship. Yet freedom of the press—a form of moral license—can also be lost if it becomes principally a vehicle for amusement. You should not remain silent if press freedom is sacrificed to sensationalism. As media critics will always hold you to account by critiquing your performance, so you have the right and duty to hold the same journalistic media to account for failure to report and elucidate matters of public concern adequately.

The temptation to recount my many personal experiences with the media is great, but it would serve little purpose other than to distract attention from this book and from more important questions of leadership. I have learned much, which can be summarized simply: If the media are able to make you a celebrity, they deny you the authority of leadership. Effort will be made by some to distract attention from this book by recounting a past sensation. Do not let this happen to you. Resist the media's efforts to reduce you to a celebrity, thereby de-

stroying you, while employing their power to inform
and educate, and thereby seek to elevate debate.

Given human frailty, there will never come a time
when either politics or press are above reproach. By elevating your own standards in the performance of the
public's business, however, you can hope to set a standard
for all those who enjoy the public trust, politicians and
press, in the pursuit of their respective responsibilities as
actors and as critics.

Notes

1. Presidents, presidential candidates, senators and representatives, all are tempted to seek press and public attention. If all
now are famous for a brief time, the temptation is great to
seek new and more bizarre ways to attract and keep the spotlight. A senator pretending to be a drug enforcement officer
may not become confused with a real drug enforcement officer, but he may be confused with an actor *pretending* to be a
drug enforcement officer.

2. *The Hero in America: A Chronicle of Hero Worship,* Dixon
Wector, 1972.

No. 24

How sycophants should be avoided

Good counsels, whensoever they come, are born of the wisdom of the prince, and not the wisdom of the prince from good counsels

THE LOYAL FRIEND AND COUNSELOR PRO-vides encouragement when the leader is tested and support in the time of trial. His faithfulness is not seasonal; he is most evident when the leader is in disfavor. Conversely, the flatterer is popularity's parasite. Success is the flame that attracts him. Daylight's harsh reality finds the fluttering sycophant gone.

The wily sycophant is not a harmless creature. Indeed, he is potentially the leader's greatest enemy. Not only is he faithless, but he also craftily seduces the leader's judgment and sometimes his conscience.

Leadership's advance bears with it the volatile component of its own destruction. Its name is hubris—the sense of endless possibility and inevitable success. Above all else the wise leader will resist the charms of hubris and its most ardent messenger, the sycophant. The sycophant is to hubris as the glass-blower is to molten glass: He breathes gently into it and inflates its shape, but leaves the center hollow.[1]

The whispered message of hubris invites the leader to presume on fortune's favor. Attention must be paid to this or you, like many before you, will sacrifice power by coming to believe that providence has chosen and will therefore protect you. Thus you begin to lose the grace that you have already secured by noble effort. Resistance to the magic spell of hubris and rejection of its messenger marks the beginning of wisdom in the leader. Beware the sycophant who whispers in your ear that you possess extraordinary virtue; select counselors whose loyalty is to the truth and not ambition. Such advisors will have conviction's authority in preventing you from pursuing a destiny you have not earned.

Choose humility as the surest antidote to hubris. Though not common, it is possible for humility to complement greatness in a leader. In an uncanny way, Abraham Lincoln used his own humanity to make himself great. The more he deprecated himself, the larger he became. The more he dressed in homespun cloth, the more the finished fabric of the statesman and general seemed stiff and harsh. The more he drew on frontier wisdom, the more he distanced himself from the aloofness of the aristocratic drawing room. He shrewdly but mystically identified himself with the greatness that is latent in every man. Knowing he is human, and therefore fallible, the humble leader will find that his actions seem all the more just for lacking hubris and ambition.

Once you temper your determination with humility, you will evoke greater and warmer support from the people as they grow to trust your sincerity. Admit error and accept blame if defeat is brought about by the actions of your subordinates. This is a curse to the sycophant and the essence of nobility in the leader.

Most of all, have sufficient surety of purpose that the sycophant's seductive song finds no ear. The strong leader feels little need for hollow praise or callow compliment; his mission is a sufficient beacon to guide him through perilous political nights. Be clear regarding your course, and the sycophant will be an anchor left well behind.

You need fear neither hubris nor the sycophant if you too identify yourself with the latent greatness in every man.

Note

1. Early success in an effort to achieve national leadership—even after much difficult struggle—is a powerful temptation to hubris. This I know from personal experience. When polls are high, contributors are available, supporters are volunteering, and the party structure is accepting, the candidate is given every reason to believe he will succeed. Some have said I took my own ultimate success for granted, but they are wrong. There were always sufficient setbacks and hurdles to prevent any permanent sense that a final victory was inevitable. And I had been around national politics long enough to know how dramatically and irrationally fortune can shift.

N°. 25

*What fortune can effect in human affairs
and how to withstand her*

*I hold it to be true that Fortune is the arbiter of one-half of
our actions, but that she still leaves us to direct the other half,
or perhaps a little less*

SINCE THE DISCOVERY OF THE SCIENTIFIC
method and the elevation of the rights of
man at the dawn of the Enlightenment, men have come
to suppose that they control their own destiny. They
have acted on the presumption that human genius has
supreme authority over nature and nature's laws, that
disaster is the product of the failure of understanding,
and that ultimately man must have dominion over all of
life. But they reckon not with human folly, and they
reckon not with fortune.

The extraordinary expansion of scientific knowledge and its offspring, technology, have brought modernity to the lives of those who control them. Diseases have been conquered, nature tamed, human toil reduced, abundance created, convenience enhanced, and consumption and amusement exalted—all this for nations blessed with natural abundance, industrial and military power, and leaders with the energy and wit to take advantage of scientific invention. But science knows no moral authority, and fortune is a trickster and a harlot.

The great age of science has produced weapons that recognize no distinction between combatant and innocent, chemicals that overwhelm the processes of nature, and forces of propulsion greater than the forces of gravity. Time forms an elliptical curve, and theories of relativity replace moral absolutes. But the greatest human folly occurs when the methods of science are applied to ultimate human adventures. Today quantitative analytical instruments—polls, voter analyses, manipulative advertising strategies, and so forth—are employed in attempt to conquer that most capricious of human endeavors, the political process. But politics, being subject to human unpredictability and fortune's whims, resists scientific quantification.

Fortune crowns the leader one day and crushes him the next. The leader either conquers fortune or is conquered by her, but neither victory is permanent, for the struggle is never over. Sometimes called circumstance but more nearly called fate, fortune is the sum and substance of all that life confronts us with, but which confronts the leader most of all because he acts for the nation. Therefore how fortune treats the leader—and how the leader responds—affects more than himself. Great nations are seldom steered off course even by powerful or willful leaders, but the nation pays a heavy price when a leader responds to fortune wrongly. Thirty years later the Vietnam war still divides America; twenty years later the mistrust of Watergate still lingers heavily. When great ill fortune shows a tragic face, as with the assassination of John Kennedy, we seek a greater cause to justify fortune's enormous consequence.[1] Neither wealth nor power can protect us from fortune's trickery.

Our instructor, Machiavelli, believed that Fortune leaves us to direct half, or perhaps a little less, or our actions. Whether half or more, how we direct that portion depends upon our virtue or valor: "Fortune, who shows her power where valor has not prepared to resist her . . . turns her forces where she knows that barriers and defenses [of virtue] have not been raised to constrain her." But virtue alone is no guarantee of success: "She [Fortune] often holds the good under her feet/raises the wicked." Fortune assumed many images for Machiavelli—a woman, the eagle, a river, the wheel, stars, winds, games—and, according to one biographer, many meanings: "fortune (success) consists in having the fortune (good luck) to vary with fortune (the times), none of which would you have were not the occasion extended you by Fortune (the deity)".[2]

Fortune can sometimes be conquered, but only by the leader with great virtue. Virtue's qualities include reason, prudence, courage, and military skill. Beyond Machiavelli, however, I believe a leader must also possess wisdom, energy and vision. Wisdom produces perspective, and thus humility. Energy provides the strength to challenge and subjugate fortune. Vision distinguishes the genuine leader from those who merely claim the title; it is the quality fortune finds most difficult to overcome. All these qualities, together with moral purpose, form the substance of virtue. Fortune cannot always be overcome, but when it can it is by the leader with virtue's qualities. It is possible to be virtuous without conquering fortune, but it is not possible to conquer fortune without being virtuous.

Fortune works her will against all who would lead. To conquer fortune through wit, audacity, and will is to qualify for greatness. Fortune favors the brave; to challenge fortune by seeking to lead is to cast the die with destiny. The leader successful in a duel with fortune (which is but a definition of a campaign for national office) acquires for himself the opportunity of elevating the aspirations of the nation. At the same time, he also guarantees a continuing struggle with fortune on a higher plane.

Fortune flourishes where leadership is weak. Unsubjugated by the virtuous leader, fortune works evil as readily as good. To conquer fortune is to master one's own destiny, which is the *sine qua non* of the leader. Only the leader who has conquered fortune is bold enough to harness science to the restoration of nature, liberate economic energies for the benefit of all, secure weapons in their arsenals, and negotiate tranquility among nations. If you are fortune's subject, you are not the nation's governor.

The great struggles to subdue and capture fortune, which you must carry out in the public arena, are never over. You must enter that arena every day, and some days you will lose. How you deal with defeat will mark you for leadership even more than how you deal with victory. Many who claim leadership do so by avoiding contests with fortune. Great leaders welcome it. To conquer fortune, though, is not simply achieving power and working one's will. Adolf Hitler rose above fortune for a brief time and then was crushed by her. Joseph Stalin can be said to have conquered fortune during his life, but the destruction of his form of totalitarianism represented fortune's victory over him in death. For a democratic leader, conquering fortune means achieving a state of spirit that rises above vicissitudes, focuses attention on the national good, and calls upon the native patriotism in most Americans to contribute to the country's renewal.

Too many mistakenly think leadership can be taken

by stealth—that it is enough to acquire the office, and the office itself will provide the leader's strength. Nothing could be more in error. True leadership is something the leader brings to the office, not something he takes from it.

Here is the difference between power and leadership: It is quite possible to have power and be no leader. It is sometimes possible to be a leader and have no power. It is not possible that power alone creates a leader. It is not possible that one without the strength, wisdom, vision, and integrity of leadership will acquire them simply by virtue of having assumed an office.

Authentic leadership creates its own fortune.

Notes

1. Thus the endless search for a greater cause or a more potent conspiracy to account for the assassination of John Kennedy.

   2. *Machiavelli in Hell,* Sebastian de Grazia, 1989 (winner of the Pulitzer Prize).

N⁰· 26

An exhortation to liberate America from the barbarians

It is seen how she entreats God to send someone who shall deliver her from these wrongs and barbarian insolencies. It is seen also that she is ready and willing to follow a banner if only someone will raise it.

POLITICIANS WHO FIND CAREERS IN WARNING of barbarians at America's gates know neither history nor the devices of human folly. The great danger to America is not derived from foreign cultures seeking to impose their values from without. This fallacy demonizes an external foe while obscuring a more critical truth. The barbarian is already within the gate and has for some time occupied the city.

For our barbarians are homegrown and span the political spectrum from left to right. They divide citizen from citizen and races, genders, and ethnic groups from each other. They sever humanity's roots in nature. They squander our children's heritage and despoil the earth. They worship modernity's materialistic consumerism. They despise the cultural and civil institutions, including the institutions of governance, that have made our nation great. They seek to impose fundamentalist economic, political, or social values on others. They deconstruct belief systems, corrupt social and cultural values for the sake of shock, amusement, and profit, and sacrifice academic integrity on the altar of political correctness.

Do not be misled. Our late 20th century barbarians are elite, sophisticated, well eduated—and selfish. They are finely tailored, well spoken, belong to the best clubs— and arrogant. They constitute our political class. They talk to us (or to themselves) on Sunday morning television, telling us whom we can trust, and forming our opinions on the issues of the day. They believe themselves entitled to select our leadership. Our barbarians harbor secret contempt for the lives and hopes of average Americans. Their loyalty is hollow. They love power more than country. They are false patriots.

Today's pin-striped barbarians are faintly bored by the hard choices facing most Americans. The country's destiny is reduced by them to calculated moves on a political chessboard, where the fate of this or that politician is deemed more interesting than the future of our children. They pass elegantly and disdainfully through halls of power, through boardroom, newsroom, and congressional caucus room, with the cynical air of corrupt medieval courtesans.

Barbarians are all those who corrode the spirit of national unity and civility necessary to achieve national restoration and the next stage in the fulfillment of the democratic ideal. For despite democracy's victory in the Cold War, there are reasons to question the inevitable triumph of Western Enlightenment and radical market liberalism throughout the world, especially since their dependence upon the technological pillage of nature has reaped enduring havoc and since their increasingly materialistic view of human happiness too much confines the human spirit. If enlightened humanism as a governing principle and value system is further eroded by forces of modern reductionist culture, fundamentalism, and materialism, what will it mean for such pivotal notions as intergenerational responsibility, multiculturalism, and racial and ethnic tolerance? Are not random urban murder and tribal genocide but parallel manifestations of this impending breakdown? Now that the age of Enlightenment may be coming to its close, like the Reformation and the Renaissance before it, consider the political implications rendered by potential future rejection of such fundamental liberal assumptions as pluralistic institutions, humanistic values, confidence in the scientific method, mastery of nature, consensus achieved by reason, the materialistic ethic, the assumption of human progress, and even enlightened self-government.[1]

The Enlightenment's last legacies—radical market liberalism and democratic government, both now based upon the premise of unlimited economic growth—are about to be tested for the first time by prolonged economic stagnation and, in some venues, economic contraction. The preliminary signs of disintegration in Western democracies such as Italy and Japan, and quasi-democracies such as Mexico and Korea, and rising public discontent in "stable" democracies such as Germany, France, Britain, and even the United States, signal the decline and approaching end of a political religion whose central object of worship is markets and whose highest claim to faith is in materialism. History may show that America's greatest barbarians were simply not those who divided and captured our society, but those in the chambers of politics and halls of commerce who gambled her great patrimony on games of chance in the casinos of the global markets.[2]

Today's conservatism suffers from this fatal flaw: its economics are at war with its professed social values. The hope of unrestricted economic growth and "progress" embodied in the radical market-liberal ideal fits well with a materialistic age. But it is bound to trammel human and natural values in the interest of unbridled consumption. Worst of all, it offers to our progeny a hollow, nihilistic destiny. The conundrum of modern political conservatism is that its superstitious worship of market forces brings about the disruption of the very families and communities that it claims to revere. For the destructive gales of unrestricted markets bring social and economic insecurity, dislocation, crime, and eventually, rightist politics.

Likewise, redistributive social liberalism has foundered on the shoals of stagnant economics and the hollow promise of materialistic comfort as man's highest aspiration. The citizens' demands on the state now exceed the state's ability to meet them. The bankruptcy of modern ideologies, and therefore political parties, produces massive public discontent with government and political "leaders." The modern industrial myth of increasing economic security through unlimited expansion has run its course.

I would propose to you a new idea of leadership, which I will call *patrimonial*. This leadership ideal draws moral force from its belief in a contract among generations. The present generation owes a duty to the forebears to preserve the best of their heritage and traditions, and it owes an equal duty to its children to transmit that patrimony at least as sound again.[3] The conveyance of a cultural, economic, legal, and natural heritage to future generations is a society's most sacred duty, and it presupposes a responsibility-based, rather than a rights-based, national ethic. The natural rights of man are best protected by a duty-conscious nation. As leader, your greatest task must be to restore the collective moral sense of responsibility for the patrimony of future generations. This is the surest means of restoring genuine patriotism.[4]

Your task is compounded by the Enlightenment's rationalist–scientific plundering of the natural heritage, by the increasingly violent legacy of racism, by the consumerist ethic, and by the nation's drift toward a dis-integrated society. All these forces make war on a collective sense of patrimonial responsibility.

Despite these obstacles, however, patrimonial leadership will begin the historic process of forcing rational choice among incommensurables. It will force citizens to accept limits on both public services and on consumption of natural and fiscal resources. Such limits are required of a mature people concerned with their children's heritage. Patrimonial leadership forces a public distinction between liberty and plunder, freedom and license. It insists on a recognition of the limitation of unrestrained markets to recognize and protect the long-term national interest and the public good. It teaches that our children's inheritance may not be best protected by this rational choice of economic man. It insists that the interests of progeny be represented in every political and economic debate. It abhors our present pattern of settlements in the political marketplace reached by power structures and interest groups reflecting only their own immediate demands without concern for future generations.

Herein lies the bankruptcy of current ideology. Neither liberalism's insistence on reason, social justice, and rights, nor conservatism's worship of tradition, legal justice, and privilege, take account of patrimonial responsibility. Since these ideologies are based upon an old industrial-growth ideal that no longer suffices, it is incumbent upon you to create a new ideal, one that can become the fountain of new value systems, new ideologies, and ultimately new public policies and programs.

As the era of *quantity* exhausts itself, a new ideal that celebrates *quality* must emerge. The ideal of quality is based upon relationships—each of us with our neighbors (the human community), all of us with nature (the community of nature), and each of us with our children (the future community). The central organizing principle of this new ideal must be to create and preserve the highest quality culture as our children's patrimony. From this, all economic and social policies should flow. The guiding principle is sufficiency rather than excess.

The political tools required to create a new patrimonial leadership based upon notions of quality and sufficiency are genius, charisma, and hope. *Genius* is required to distinguish the elements of a quality-based culture, design new precepts for economic security, devise a new definition of community premised on parity among genders, races, and ethnic groups, and, through force of idea, to command the ground of debate. This sort of genius is more the consequence of identity with the national interest, i.e., the truest patriotism, than of any intellectual superiority. *Charisma* results as well from embodying the national interest and the moral force of patrimonial leadership. Charisma encompasses a peculiar vitality or energy crucial to command the field of national debate. Apart from ordinary politicians, the charismatic leader is recognized by his clarity of vision and his purity of purpose in protecting the national interest. *Hope* is the vital, optimistic energy that inspires the people to believe their children's future will be promising and bright. Hope is the intuitive faith, inspired by the genius of the charismatic leader, that concrete measures taken today may secure the cultural and natural heritage of their children.

This new ideal of patrimonial leadership can also be the basis of a new myth for the post-Enlightenment age. This myth envisions the earth as a singular craft adrift on the cosmic ocean, nature as the ground and sustenance of human life, and the human race as an evolving multifarious species in progress toward restoring its natural matriarchal roots. Imagine, if you will, all these forces as embodied by the astronaut who uniquely has seen the beauty, harmony, and unity of earth, the native American who can negotiate a new contract between humanity and nature, and an ethnic female activist who can reconcile breaches between genders and among racial

tribes. These three archetypal figures form the first cho-
rus in the new national myth. The result of this new
myth or national narrative can be the reformation of
civil institutions to better serve legitimate citizen needs,
a renaissance of scientific, cultural, and humanistic cre-
ativity, a reconciliation of races and genders and of all
humanity with nature, and the redemption of our national pride and spirit.

The barbarians within our gates, knowingly or un-
knowingly, prosper on our nation's confusion and drift.
The new patrimonial leadership will banish these false
patriots by raising the formidable banner of national
unity. Where Machiavelli advocated the use of mystery,
fear, and authority to coerce behavior in the interest of
the state, you must use genius, charisma, and hope to
unify the people around a new national myth as a narrative for twenty-first-century national life.

You have asked for my counsel, and I have provided it
to the best of my ability. Some will call these meditations idealistic and impractical, but that is what many
still say about our country itself. I am not ashamed to be
known as an idealist. Democracy itself is an ideal that
can never be fully realized but one that exercises a powerful attraction to the minds and hearts of people every-
where.

Our country is adrift. It urgently awaits a guide and
the fulfillment of its destiny. Fearful that it has no new
frontiers and entering late middle age, America has no
great purpose or unifying cause. It preoccupies itself

with amusement and entertainment and begins to divide among clans, tribes, and gangs. Give the restoration of the bonds of trust between yourself and the people your whole attention. Do not follow the course of politics as usual. Make your whole course that of the national interest and the commonwealth. The national interest is real and it is transcendent. Like the ideal of democracy itself, it is a torch whose brightness you must restore.

The very position of leader will require you to be always in the public arena. You cannot and should not seek to remain above it. You will be required to compromise and conciliate. You will have to negotiate with those you neither trust nor respect. Make them profit by your example of decency and honor. By that example, you will restore honor to political leadership. You will restore respect to public service. You will restore nobility to the governance of America.

Pass that torch to the next generation and secure your greatness.

Notes

1. Consider this evidence of corrosion: pluralistic institutions central to democracy are threatened in many countries, including Russia, by authoritarian capitalism whose most recent model was Pinochet's Chile; humanistic values are rejected in Bosnia and Rwanda in favor of trans-tribal slaughter; the scientific method is poised on the threshold of the

186

brave new Huxleian world of genetic mutation; mastery of nature is achieved at the cost of entire rainforests and global warming; the congressional budget "debate" of 1995-96 makes a mockery of concensus achieved by reason; the materialistic ethic is producing generations of young people with little idealism and no great cause; for every Gandhi or Martin Luther King there is a Saddam Hussein or a Slobodan Milosovich to question human progress; and the torch of enlightened self-government does not burn brightly in a nation half of whose citizens cannot trouble themselves to vote.

2. The oft-quoted prophet of modern radical market liberalism, Adam Smith, was much more conscious of the limits of markets than his latter-day apostles. For example: "There are some inconveniences arising from a commercial spirit. The first we shall mention is that it confines the views of men."

3. The concept of intergenerational contract, and thus patrimonial leadership, is from the notable conservative Edmund Burke, who spoke of it as a partnership between generations.

4. Originally from the Latin root for father, and defined as inheritance from a male ancestor, patrimony here is meant to include both maternal and paternal inheritance, that is to say, the entire legacy of a culture.